ANDBOOK on

CHOOSING your child's EDUCATION

HANDBOOK on

CHOOSING your

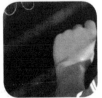

child's EDUCATION

A Personalized Plan for Every Age and Stage

General Editor

Maria Hernandez Ferrier, Ed.D.

Tyndale House Publishers, Inc.
Carol Stream, Illinois

A Focus on the Family book published by
Tyndale House Publishers, Inc., Carol Stream, Illinois 60188

TYNDALE and Tyndale's quill logo are registered trademarks of Tyndale House Publishers, Inc.

Editor: Marianne Hering
Cover design: Julie Chen
Cover photo credits: Boy at blackboard © by David Buffington/Getty Images. All rights reserved. Girl drawing © by Ingram Publishing/Getty Images. All rights reserved. Boy raising hand © by Digital Vision/Getty Images. All rights reserved. School bus © by Paul Tearle/Getty Images. All rights reserved. Books and apple © by Pamela Moore/iStockphoto. All rights reserved. Boy in green shirt © by Danish Khan/iStockphoto. All rights reserved. Girl with dark hair © by Debi Bishop/iStockphoto. All rights reserved. Graduate © by Charles Shapiro/iStockphoto. All rights reserved. Crayon © by Pamela Moore/iStockphoto. All rights reserved. Boy reading © by Anne Chelnokova/iStockphoto. All rights reserved. Pencils copyright © by Marcelo Wain/iStockphoto. All rights reserved. Boy doing homework copyright © by Chris Schmidt/iStockphoto. All rights reserved. Group of kids copyright © by Daniela Andreea Spyropoulos/iStockphoto. All rights reserved. Girl with globem copyright © by iStockphoto. All rights reserved.

Library of Congress Cataloging-in-Publication Data
Handbook on choosing your child's education : a personalized plan for every age and stage / Maria Hernandez Ferrier, editor.
     p. cm.
  Includes bibliographical references.
  ISBN-13: 978-1-58997-341-1
  ISBN-10: 1-58997-341-0
  1. School choice–United States—Handbooks, manuals, etc. I. Hernandez-Ferrier, Maria
  LB1027.9.H345 2007
  379.1'110973—dc22
                    2007000527

Printed in the United States of America
1 2 3 4 5 6 7 8 9 / 12 11 10 09 08 07

Contents

Part Three:
What's Next?

Foreword

A new day is dawning on education in America.

With the stroke of a pen our 43rd President established the No Child Left Behind Act (NCLB), the federal education law of the land, and gave you, your child's first teacher, viable options when answering the important question: *Where will my child go to school?* While our public schools still have a long way to go before fulfilling the promise of NCLB, children no longer need be trapped in failing schools and parents have rights as never before. This is a revolutionary time in education. States, school districts, and individual schools are accountable to parents and communities for the academic success of the students they serve. Parents are being educated and empowered to ask the important questions, and schools must give prompt and honest answers.

The *Handbook on Choosing Your Child's Education* will help you find what you need to make informed decisions about schooling for your child, the force that will be shaping your child's life today and in the future. You will learn about public schools, charter schools, private schools, and homeschools. This education handbook was written by seasoned teachers and authors; their experiences and advice will excite you and give a sense that you are not alone in your quest to provide your child with the best possible education.

Today many parents are not only concerned with the academic success of their children but with their spiritual development and well-being as well. And for good reason. There is a loud and visible attack on anything regarding education that includes the Christian faith and its role in education and in the establishing of our nation. Parents who do not know the U.S. constitution, the law, or their rights believe that they are helpless. But they are not!

It was our 26th president, Theodore Roosevelt, who said, "To educate a person in mind and not in morals is to educate a menace to society." President Roosevelt died in 1919 but those words resonate with us even more loudly today. The erosion of the philosophy of education, as envisioned by our founding fathers, is evident when comparing Webster's 1828 definition of education to today's definition in *Webster's New Universal Unabridged Dictionary*. The 1828 definition states, "to give children a good education in manners, arts, and science is important; to give them a religious education is indispensable; and an immense responsibility rests on parents and guardians who neglect these duties." The *Webster's New Universal Unabridged Dictionary* defines education as "the act or process of imparting or acquiring general knowledge, developing the powers of reasoning and judgment, and generally preparing oneself or others intellectually for mature life." The latter ignores the foundation upon which sound reasoning and judgment must be made if we are to remain a strong democracy.

If schools can't do it right, you, your child's most important and influential teacher, can. You can ensure that your faith and values are fostered and imprinted indelibly on your child's character. Those values will guide and direct your child from childhood through adulthood. No one is better equipped to do this than you. This book will help you in this quest.

In October 2006, President Bush said that we must improve options for parents. Yes, we must, because every morning in all 50 states, hundreds of thousands of parents unaware of their rights or without financial resources to send their children elsewhere, drop off their children at the schoolhouse door simply hoping and praying for the best.

The goal of this book is that you do not find yourself in the same dilemma as those parents. Whatever your life circumstances, you can powerfully and positively impact your child's academic, emotional, and spiritual growth.

Take the information within this book and put it to work for you. Share it with other parents. Our children need parents as advocates, and you are the most important advocate your child has.

Your child will not be left behind. Your child has you!

—Maria Hernandez Ferrier, Ed.D.

It's a New Day in Education

A New Day

by Marc Fey

*Parents have become so convinced that educators
know what is best for their children that they forget
that they themselves are really the experts.*
—MARIAN WRIGHT EDELMAN

*Come, my children, listen to me;
I will teach you the fear of the LORD.*
—PSALM 34:11

Every school day some 56 million U.S. children attend school—one their parents chose for them.[1] The educational choices facing parents today are numerous, including private Christian schools, public schools, charter schools, homeschools, and magnet schools. And that initial school choice doesn't reflect the options buried within each system, such as whether your child should participate in sports programs, after-school enrichment programs, or honors courses.

Additionally, the educational controversies facing parents today are staggering. Each day the media present news stories about the debate between evolution and intelligent design, disagreement over the "best" school models, or conflicting solutions for declining reading and math scores. Class size, funding, and English language development are additional sources of controversy.

But none of these challenges are as formidable as the one simple question facing every parent: *What is the right education choice for my child?* This book is about giving you the keys to solve the educational challenges that come your way—for the sake of your child and for your family.

My Family's Education Journey

Right now, my wife and I are satisfied with our family's education. Our three children (two sons and a daughter) attend The Classical Academy, a public charter school. Founded about 10 years ago by a group of visionary parents, the school emphasizes character development and classical education. Our sons have completed five years in the school, and generally speaking, we're happy with our children's education.

But it has certainly been an arduous journey up to this point. The road led through three years of private Christian schooling, a year of homeschooling, and a year at a neighborhood public school. Over the past nine years, my wife and I have made decisions based on finances (we couldn't afford private school tuition), options (charter versus neighborhood school), time (homeschooling versus traditional schooling), and values (spiritual training at home versus spiritual training at school).

Scriptures on Teaching Your Children

Only be careful, and watch yourselves closely so that you do not forget the things your eyes have seen or let them slip from your heart as long as you live. Teach them to your children and to their children after them. Remember the day you stood before the LORD your God at Horeb, when he said to me, "Assemble the people before me to hear my words so that they may learn to revere me as long as they live in the land and may teach them to their children." (Deuteronomy 4:9-10)

Fix these words of mine in your hearts and minds; tie them as symbols on your hands and bind them on your foreheads. Teach them to your children, talking about them when you sit at home and when you walk along the road, when you lie down and when you get up. Write them on the doorframes of your houses and on your gates. (Deuteronomy 11:18-20)

Do not exasperate your children; instead, bring them up in the training and instruction of the Lord. (Ephesians 6:4)

Perhaps you have had the same experience that my wife and I have had in making decisions about our children's education. Almost every year we find ourselves reevaluating where they are, what the kids are learning, and the options available to us. This year is especially transitional—our oldest is a high school freshman, our second child is entering middle school as a seventh grader, and our youngest is a kindergartener. So, you could say we have all the transitions covered!

In addition to my perspective on education choices, I bring 10 years of teaching high school English in California public schools, a year of teaching numerous subjects at a Christian school, and about 10 years of teaching college essay writing part-time in various settings. As a high school teacher, I coached football, baseball, and basketball, advised the yearbook staff, served as a California district mentor teacher, and worked as an English department chairperson for four years. After seven years as a pastor, I served as an education policy analyst at Focus on the Family, researching, commenting, and writing on the topic of education as it affects families around America.

So, my viewpoint is informed by beliefs developed through exposure to a variety of family and education settings and experiences. In addition, my wife and I have a tutoring business to help young people develop stronger cognitive skills. Providing families with coaching resources to help parents make decisions about their children's education, we have come to appreciate this fact: There is no single solution that applies to all families. In fact, you can say that there is a specific and unique solution for every child.

Even with my experience in the education field, I find that I still have, at times, an uncertain feeling deep down that makes me think my wife and I might not be doing all we could, or should, for our kids' education. That, of course, is the flip side to having options— *with more choices, we face more complexity.*

Each Family Has a Choice

Perhaps one of these scenarios illustrates your family's path:

Jeana, a single mother, knew her son Jared, a sophomore, was not keeping up in high school. Ever since kindergarten he'd struggled with reading. But she didn't see many options for change. The public school was the only financially viable choice for him, but the remedial help Jared had received for years through the district wasn't solving his reading problem. She tried private tutors, but they were too expensive to use on a daily basis. Jeana finally found a tutoring service that would train her to work with Jared. After several months of working with him daily, Jeana finally began to see dramatic improvement in Jared's reading comprehension. She now has hope that he will be able to succeed in college.

● ● ●

The Knudsons were having a hard time communicating with their son's first-grade teacher, who was suggesting that squirrelly Mitchell should repeat first grade. After Mitchell was tested and observed by an objective education consultant, the Knudsons decided that the last thing Mitchell needed was to repeat a grade that he was already bored with.

● ● ●

Jack and Kathryn Salas took the plunge to homeschool their four
kids, ages 5 to 14. The decision was difficult since no one in their
extended family had ever homeschooled their children, so they
did their best to overcome many of the misconceptions that came
up in conversations with their extended family. A year later, they
were exhausted but very satisfied with their renewed relationships
with their four children and the academic progress they'd seen in
their children's lives. This coming fall they are planning an educational vacation to Washington, D.C.

As the scenarios above illustrate, the education dilemmas and
options facing families are numerous, and no one solution will fit
every family. Parents have to evaluate their child's educational needs,
evaluate their long-term goals, determine which sacrifices they can
make, and take the best option available in their community.

Those decisions aren't easy to make, and often the process produces a fair amount of emotional unrest. I know from my conversations with parents, children, and educators around the country that a
lot of moms and dads share this uncertainty and indecisiveness. It isn't
that the parents are struggling with vague emotional unrest; there are
some valid reasons for these feelings of anxiety.

Real Concerns

Marilyn, whose son attends a Catholic high school in Northern California, described her challenge this way: "I send him to school, but I

feel like I am sending him into a whole other world where I don't know what is happening. If I thought it was just about what his teachers were giving him, I could handle it. But it seems his life with his friends takes up as much or more of his day than schoolwork. I sure miss the simple days of elementary school." Marilyn's experience describes many parents' experience—they feel as though they are on the outside of the education experience.

Education research today tells us that there is cause for concern. In *Beyond the Classroom: Why School Reform Has Failed and What Parents Need to Do,* researcher Laurence Steinberg summarizes the problems in our schools by noting that a large percentage of both students and parents is disengaged from the educational process. We will look at this more closely in the following chapters, but for now, this key idea of *engagement* will serve as a foundation for our approach.[2]

In March 2002, Dr. James Dobson, founder and chairman of the board of Focus on the Family, uttered words he thought he would never say. Addressing some disturbing developments in public schools on a national radio broadcast, Dr. Dobson said, "In the state of California, if I had a child there, I wouldn't put that youngster into public schools."

The comments certainly riled the education "powers that be" and created discussion from different perspectives in the debate over education.

What was lost on most of the people weighing in on the debate was this simple fact: We all agree that something drastic needs to be done to overhaul our education system. In fact, there are few things that Republicans and Democrats agree on; one of them is the need to address the frighteningly low achievement scores of American students. Everyone is reaching for answers.

It's not that we haven't spent the money. Spending since 1920 has gone from $440 per student on average (in constant 2001 school dollars) to $8,194.[3] That's over $500 billion, and 46 percent of the total federal spending budget. For this increasing investment of dollars, only 31 percent of 4th graders score "proficient" in reading. Though Americans spend more than any nation on education, our 12th graders rank 18th out of 21 countries (in the most recent comparisons) in combined math and science literacy scores.

For many parents, however, the most important factor in American public schools is the issue of safety. The availability of drugs and alcohol and the intense culture of peer pressure present far more threatening challenges than poor academics. This crisis of safety is described in surveys that show almost half of American high school students (47 percent) felt their schools were becoming more violent, and one in five were afraid to go to the bathroom.[4] As parents, we want to know our kids are safe—physically, emotionally, and spiritually. And in the education setting, a child cannot learn until he or she feels safe and secure.

These challenges in our education system are a reflection of our culture, and we find them at every turn. So, our task here is to evaluate the critical information we need to make the best decisions for our children and family, with our eyes wide open about the challenges around us, while also not fearing or dreading the decision-making process.

So, this education guide is about the following practical actions:

- Collecting the information you need to make an informed and wise choice
- Making decisions based on the circumstances and seasons of your family life—whether you have just moved to a new neighborhood, for example, or you've learned your child has special learning needs or challenges
- Evaluating the education your child is receiving and helping you to decide if it is working or not, based on the criteria that you choose

Your Journey on the Road to Education Decisions

All of this brings to mind one backpacking trip I went on with a friend in college. We were in a wilderness area of the Sierra Nevada mountains, trying to find the trailhead at the beginning of a five-day trip. For some reason, we couldn't find it. Sure, we had our topographical map, but truth be told, we had never had to actually use a topo map in all the trips we had taken before.

But this trip was an exception. After the first half day of walking in what felt like a huge circle, we finally admitted that we were completely off trail. By midday, we were exhausted, disheartened, and most importantly, still not sure where we were.

So, what did my friend and I do? As we sat down to regather ourselves, we pulled out the crisp, unused topographical map, and laid the compass over the map. Next, trying to recall the lessons I had been taught about how to use a topo map, I looked for and found a peak that I recognized. With the map, the compass, and the recognition of a couple of key landmarks, we finally started to understand where we were. And at that, we could get on with the journey.

Knowing where we are and finding our way over today's education landscape is a lot like my backpacking experience. We start out with the best intentions, head in the right direction, but the trail gets confusing and complicated, and then we realize we're not where we thought we would be. During the course of the book, consider us your traveling partner over the often unfamiliar ground of your child's education.

We won't tell you the "right answer" because only you can determine what that is, but we will help you make decisions based on your God-given authority as a parent, your right to determine what is best for your child, and your vision of your child's growth and development—so that your child becomes all that God intends for him or her to be. So, I propose that over the next 11 chapters, you use this guide as a map to navigate through unfamiliar territory—right into the center of the best education choice for your child.

The Take-Charge Parent

Since the 1960s, parents have been taught a dangerous subliminal message: *Just put your kids on the big yellow school bus, and we'll take care of their education from there.* No one says this out loud, of course. But if you look closely, the message is there in most of the education groups, including the National Education Association (NEA), American Federation of Teachers (AFT), American Association of School Administrators (AASA), and education colleges across the country.

What does this mean practically for you and me? It is our job to take full control of our children's education by making decisions that are in the best interest of our children and family. To do that effectively, we must become parents who take charge of every aspect of our child's education, eventually becoming the expert in what is best for our children.

To become a *take-charge parent*, it is important to understand that the Bible presents at least five principles about our responsibility to shape and form our children's lives through biblical education. In fact, these five premises serve as an underpinning for a philosophy of education that has framed our work at Focus on the Family. Here are those foundational premises.

God, the Creator, is Lord over *all* of creation. God rejoices in what He has created. His desire is for the restoration of creation from the consequences of sin in the world.

God loves the brilliance of diversity and the blessing of unity. As a result, He is actively pursuing the reconciliation of all things to Himself.

God loves to see change and growth. In creation around us as well as in our lives, God has designed life for growth, through specific times and seasons.

God loves us and relates to us as a Father to His child. In that context, He desires for us to grow, to mature, and ultimately to take our place in His larger story of creation.

God seeks for us to grow in wisdom. Since it is His great desire to share His kingdom with us, God desires for us to grow in wisdom and knowledge.

Below you will find three pillars of the philosophy of education that drives Focus on the Family's activity in this area. I encourage you to read what is presented here and then tailor it to your own family and calling. Use this as a jumping-off point for your own beliefs and convictions.

EDUCATION PRINCIPLE 1:
Education of the individual is foundational for developing humanity toward its fullest potential.

How do I apply this education principle in a practical way? Let's take a look at the book of Genesis for some answers. In the Garden of Eden, God *instructed* Adam with specific directions about tending the garden, and later, in his relationship with Eve. Interestingly, God's initiative to teach Adam about his relationship to life shows His care and love for Adam. With those instructions come increased responsibility (naming the animals, living beside the temptation of the two trees) and blessing (the provision of the garden and the intimacy of relationship with God and Eve).

Parents who are serious about this first principle make great sacrifices in order to educate their children. A biblical education starts with a commitment on the part of the parents to answer the call of God to impart life principles to their children.

At Focus on the Family, we hold to a "high view of education," which we share with moms and dads who have answered that call. Interestingly, research tells us that educational success occurs when all involved in the education process "value consistency, communities, and social capital." These are researcher terms for *trust*. Effective families build trust between family members through meaningful, ongoing interaction. Thus, when we develop the individual to his or her potential, by extension we develop society.

EDUCATION PRINCIPLE 2:
At its foundation, education consists of equipping the child's mind and shaping the child's character, which together result in developing the architecture of the soul.

Let's examine the Garden of Eden story again. Adam was held responsible for the instructions that God had given him. In other words, there was a clear, causal relationship between God's words and Adam's actions. Why? Because God knew that the very personhood of Adam was at stake—what Adam did came directly from what he believed about who God was and who he was.

I am reminded that God's trust in us comes from His desire to have men and women who worship Him freely. With that freedom comes the potential for relationship with God, illustrating the kind of interdependence we see among the Father, the Son, and the Holy Spirit.

Moms and dads who understand this principle link educational outcomes to a realistic definition of progress and achievement. Achievement occurs in the meaningful context of relationship with others, especially with mom and dad. The watchword of the day in education is *accountability* (testing, school choice, standards, etc.). For effective parents, the formation of their child's mind and character is worked out every day, each lesson interwoven with the formation of what the child thinks and how the child acts—mind and character. Parents are singularly situated and called to provide this kind of accountability; *it is not just who the child is but also who the child is becoming.*

Developing Your List of Priorities and Non-negotiables

Since "education choice" is available today in most communities, it is important for you to be clear about your education priorities and steadfast non-negotiables—in other words, those values and education components that are necessary for you to make the right choices.

Also, it is important to remember that your non-negotiables may change over your child's school life, since the needs of a high school student are different from the needs of an elementary student. Finally, please keep in mind that rarely, if ever, will you be able to guarantee that all of your priorities are present in your education choice. All the more reason to remember that as the primary educator in your child's life, you will be providing in other ways what isn't available in the education setting you choose.

Examples of priorities and non-negotiables:

• My child needs a safe school where bullying is not tolerated.

• We want a school where drug and alcohol use is not a problem.

EDUCATION PRINCIPLE 3:
Finally, and most important, Focus on the Family believes that the most important educators in a child's life are his or her parents.

I notice in the chapters of Genesis following Adam and Eve's fall that they are absent in the lives of their children. The alienation that Adam experienced between himself and God is the heritage of all families today. The consummate challenge in educating our children is to break through the distance and isolation that can occur

- My child needs a character-based education.
- I am willing to do anything for my child to have a Christian education.
- I want control over the information my child receives about evolution.
- I want diverse student activities (band, sports) available to my child.
- My child needs academic rigor in high school (ranking, availability of advanced placement courses, etc.).
- My child needs remediation resources, tools that will help me shore up weaker areas in his education.
- Without top-notch special education resources, my child probably won't succeed.
- Since I work two jobs, the location of school and transportation concerns are key to me.
- We want a school where I can know the parents of my child's friends.
- I am most concerned about the cost of my child's education.

in human relationships, and in particular, families.

When the parents see themselves as the primary educators in their children's lives, a relationship is built that has to "work."

I know that in my own teaching experience in schools, I can tell when what I am doing day-to-day is working or is not working. Parents who see their daily role as educator spend the time working with their children to develop their minds and character.

In a large part, the rest of this education guide is all about helping you step into that role as the primary teacher in your child's life, whether you decide to homeschool or place your child in a traditional classroom setting, public or private, Christian or secular.

As we tackle this challenge to *engage* our children and their education, we will specifically discuss:

- How to communicate specific messages to your children— both intentionally and indirectly—about school and about learning, so that your children come to understand the importance and value of school

- How to look at and modify your own behavior as a parent in order to positively influence your child's view of education, thus serving as the most important role model in your child's life

- How to develop an atmosphere in the home environment through your parenting style that supports and enhances your child's success at school

- How to make sure your intentions truly match your actions over the long haul of your children's education

So let's get out the map and begin the journey. It's a long one, and we have no time to waste!

The Changing Face of Education

by Marc Fey

Education is not the filling of a pail,
but the lighting of a fire.
—WILLIAM BUTLER YEATS

When the foundations are being destroyed,
what can the righteous do?
—PSALM 11:3

How did we get here?" I hear this question from parents around the country after I've given a talk about the state of education today, and the question is usually accompanied by a look of frustration. Everyone wants to know what went wrong with the grand idea of educating every child in America.

The result is a sense of resignation among many parents; they believe their options are limited, and that there is little they can do to direct their child's education. Of course, we didn't get here overnight. What started out as a pretty good idea—a local community collaborating to support the education needs of all the children—has in many cases gone awry. It's working in some places, and not in many others. That is why it's important to understand how we got to the place we find ourselves.

In fact, to understand our current education challenges and make the best choices for our children, we're going to return to our analogy

DID YOU KNOW?

The earliest settlements in America, including the Virginia Company at Jamestown and the Separatists at Plymouth Colony, established colonies whose religious convictions dominated their view of education. In fact, by 1635 the first schools were established: The Latin Grammar School in Massachusetts and the first "free" school in Virginia, followed by Harvard College in 1636. These schools were primarily founded to educate "sons of certain social classes who were destined for leadership positions in the church, the state, or the courts."[1] Schools were important to our forefathers, as they are important to us today.

of the topographical map from chapter 1. There are high points and low ones, but like a good topographical map, the important point is to understand the big picture so you know how to get to where you are going.

Before we talk about how you can take back control of your child's education, a quick topographical flyover of our country's education history will help you better understand the challenges we face today. We'll look at six basic areas—understanding, of course, that this overview is simplified to highlight the aspects of history most important to our discussion. Nevertheless, this will be a good overview, providing context for the questions we will answer.

Scene 1: The Landscape of Community Responsibility— America's Education Roots in the 1600s and 1700s

Imagine a Friday evening at the end of a hard week, and you have invited all of your neighbors over to tackle a common challenge. You are all new to the area, you're working together to get the local economy up and going so that it will provide for your families, and even though you are busy and tired at the end of every day, you know that the key to your neighborhood's long-term success is your children's education. That's what this evening's meeting is about—how you can all work together to provide the education your children need while also attending to the demands of every day's work.

Your gathering on this Friday night is probably not a lot different from what our founding fathers (and their families) must have had. Knowing that the future of their communities rested to a large extent on the kinds of leaders they raised their children to be, they founded our country's earliest schools to provide for this need.

The roots of our country's education systems shared this value—a community collaborated, bringing their best resources together to provide for the children's moral and intellectual development. At the outset, public schools, locally controlled and operated, met this need.

In fact, legislation also reflected this sense of responsibility that early American communities had toward education. As early as 1642, the Massachusetts Bay School Law required that parents ensured that their children knew the laws of the commonwealth and the principles of their religion. In other words, schools made sure that kids became good citizens.

Parents also chipped in to pay for the education that they were providing to all the children in the township. Most Americans today would be surprised to find out that the Massachusetts Law of 1647 decreed that every town of at least 50 families "hire a schoolmaster who would teach the town's children to read and write and that all towns of at least 100 families should have a Latin grammar school-master who would prepare students to attend Harvard College."[2] Our early American forefathers saw education as the context for teaching

A Take-Away Point from History

Understand that educating your child, though ultimately your responsibility, is also the collaborative effort of a whole community. We need each other to provide for the educational needs of our children.

faith and morality through the developing of skills like reading and writing. So committed were they to this idea that they wrote into law a way to ensure that education was valued, and they were willing to pay for it.

Scene 2: The Landscape of Moral and Spiritual Training—the 1700s in American Education

Parents wanted schools to teach moral behavior and spiritual maturity. Even though much of the 1700s emphasized ideas influenced by the European Enlightenment such as secularism, science, and human reason, American schools provided a strong moral and religious education

DID YOU KNOW?

As much as we might disdain its involvement today, the fact is government was involved in education from our country's earliest days. Early legislation, however, reflected the American family's values and religious beliefs as the purpose of education. In the Northwest Ordinance (1787), which limited the expansion of slavery into newer territories, Act 3 of the document began, "Religion, morality, and knowledge, being necessary to good government and the happiness of mankind, schools and the means of education shall forever be encouraged."[3] More practically, it stipulated that a section of land in every township of each new state be reserved for the support of education. So the ongoing battles over education that are played out in the news we read every day have their roots in America's early convictions in the value of education and the community's corporate responsibility to educate its youth.

for its students. But the confrontation was mounting between this strong emphasis on what the family valued and the multiple approaches to education coming from the European Enlightenment.

One well-known model began to gain traction: Benjamin Franklin's English Academy (later the University of Pennsylvania), which was based widely on Enlightenment philosophy. Thomas Jefferson's two-track system for "the laboring and the learned" introduced the notion that education serves different outcomes for different students. If you have followed the heated debate in our schools today, you will recognize this basic dichotomy—education for the job market (laboring) and for higher learning (the learned).

Even with the influence of the Enlightenment starting to infringe on the American system, there was still not a lot of debate about curriculum in schools during the 1700s. Rather, there was a consistency of instruction provided, for example, by texts like Noah Webster's widely used *A Grammatical Institute of the English Language*. It consisted of three volumes: a spelling book, a grammar book, and a reader. For over one hundred years, the volumes taught children how to read, spell, and pronounce words. In fact, the spelling volume, later renamed the *American Spelling Book* and often called the *Blue-Backed Speller* for its distinctive cover, has never been out of print!

Scene 3: Treacherous Educational Philosophies at Odds—the 1800s and 1900s

The public education system as we know it today, structurally speaking, took shape in the 1800s, with the founding of the first public high school in 1837 in Boston. This school was characterized by an emphasis on citizenship, community support, and character education, as well as rigorous academic training.

You could accurately say that in these early days, family and community values drove the content of instruction and the culture of the school. For example, carved on two statues located at this first school in Boston were these phrases: "Service to mankind is honor and achievement" and "The aim of every schoolboy is to become a man of honor and achievement."[4] Public education was indeed deeply rooted in the convictions of the strong moral obligation to service and honor.

While the structure of our schools today was taking shape during the nineteenth century, a diametrically opposed philosophy about what was the purpose of public education was brewing. As we

DID YOU KNOW?

We are a good hundred years down the road from Deweyan educational philosophy, which was shaped by evolutionary naturalism and stood in direct opposition to classical foundations built on absolute truth. His philosophy constructed a nontheistic image of God that discounted the notion of the personal God of the Bible. In other words, Dewey was the strongest and earliest force in proposing a secular education system. This story is full of ironic twists, including one interesting fact that would be hard for many to believe: At the turn of the nineteenth century, the NEA (today a liberal and at times antifamily organization) believed that religious education was a part of the public school experience.

entered the twentieth century, John Dewey's "theory of experience" gave traction to the movement of progressivism, a reaction against what he called the authoritarian, strict, knowledge-delivery systems of the nineteenth century. Instead, Dewey thought that education must take into account the unique differences between students. While this education philosophy did challenge teachers to be sensitive to the individual learning needs of each student, it also set the stage for individual needs to be deemed more important than community needs and outcomes. Is it any mystery then, that in many settings today we see learning disconnected from personal responsibility?

A Take-Away Point from History

"What's this all got to do with the decisions that I need to make about my child's education?" you might be asking. Here is the point. The heritage of education philosophy based on Deweyan naturalism often bypassed the practical theological questions about, for example, the persistence of human evil. That one point is very important, because if a teacher believes that every child in the classroom is basically good, he or she will adjust discipline practices in accordance. The fact is Dewey's views of man and God continue to influence education theory today. Your understanding of this heritage, particularly if your child attends a public school, will help you discern the practices of classroom teachers and administrators as you are alert to the negative influences to which your child might be exposed.

Scene 4: The Deep Canyons of Secular Humanism in the 1960s and 1970s

The 1960s was a decade of highs and lows. As with most philosophical movements, the error was often in the swing to the extreme. As we look back on the educational history of the United States, it is evident that we have had many good ideas and many bad ideas. When the 1960s exploded onto the scene, key pieces were in place that contributed to the complicated education ethos we have today.

Most important, what the 1960s did was to move the cultural war *inside* the four walls of the school, starting first with the universities, and later with secondary and finally elementary schools. We all remember, either from our history classes, personal experience, or

DID YOU KNOW?

Prominent educators included Horace Mann, Mary Lyon, Hervey Wilbur, and Booker T. Washington, who contributed to the expansion of education as a public institution. By 1839 the first state-funded teacher training college opened; in 1852 the first mandatory student attendance laws were adopted; and in 1857 the National Teachers Association (now the National Education Association) was founded. Each of these pieces would become a key component of the education system that we inherited in the twentieth century, and would do much to explain the highly centralized structure of public schools today. What started out as local education would soon become national public education.

movies like *Forrest Gump,* the confrontational protests, sit-ins, and other political activities of universities and colleges.

Notice what the effect of this was—the focus of school activities moved from academic training to social commentary and revolution. In particular, Marxist theories dominated nearly every discipline as professors and many of their student protégées promoted social and political agendas. Understand the key point here: Just as dangerous as these ideas was the fact that the battle moved from outside of the four walls of the school to inside.

Though adults have a tendency to look at the next generation as more rebellious and independent than their own, certainly there is no

DID YOU KNOW?

In 1962, the U.S. Supreme Court decision in Engel v. Vitale made pre-scribed, teacher-led, and school-sponsored prayer (and many other varia-tions of religious expression) in public schools unlawful. In 1963, however, the first black student was admitted to the University of Mississippi, finally breaking the race barrier in a Southern university. The Civil Rights Act (1964) and then the Coleman Report (1966) addressed the importance of equal opportunities for all students, no matter the student's race, color, reli-gion, or national origin. The Coleman Report showed that the strongest factors in student achievement were not inequitable funding, but family socioeconomic status and the backgrounds and aspirations of other stu-dents in the school. As a result, school busing was one policy decision made on the basis of the Coleman Report findings.

debate that the 1960s "normalized" the rejection of authority and the previous generation's code. Parental authority has been under attack ever since. The absence of parent involvement in the public school system today is, at least in part, the legacy that the 1960s and 1970s gave us. The irony, of course, is that the grandparents of today's schoolchildren are to a large extent the very ones who rejected their parents' authority.

As a result, in the 1960s and 1970s the academic curriculum became secondary to social concerns, political agendas, and newfangled teaching methods. What the education system hosted was a long run of educational trends and gimmicks. In fact, the social commentary agenda of school leaders actually bred a disdain for intellectualism as an expression of "the establishment." With the focus on the individual student and politics of education, we lost our way. Diane Ravitch, author of *Left Back: A Century of Failed School Reforms,* describes this period of time where anti-intellectualism dominated educators' thinking and practices:

> As the academic curriculum lost its importance as the central focus of the public school system, the schools lost their anchor, their sense of mission, their intense moral commitment to the intellectual development to each child. Once that happened, education reform movements would come and go with surprising rapidity, almost randomly, each leaving its mark behind in the schools. Over time, as this happened, educators forgot how to say "no," even to the loopiest notions of what schools were for.[5]

So, today we still joke about "the new math" and other pop-education concepts and methods like outcome-based education, self-esteem-focused theory, whole language instruction, and a host of others. Yet their legacy lives on. Now we wonder, "Exactly why should my child read Shakespeare?" Never mind trying to defend the core educational value of reading the Bible in a public school. We have certainly lost our understanding of education's purpose. As a parent in charge of your child's education, be sure that your child's experience stays focused on the main thing—academic, character and/or spiritual, and social development of your child.

Scene 5: Wide Stretches in the Education Landscape— Big Government from the 1970s to 2001

The word that best describes the 1980s and 1990s would be *money*. More than at any time in our history, we spent an astonishing amount of money on trying to solve the problems all experts agree pervade our school system. Based on the most current statistics, recent numbers showed government dollars on education included $455 billion spent in 2002-2003. Of that total, elementary and sec-

---

A Take-Away Point from History

Help your child's school and teachers stay focused on the bull's-eye of education by resisting the activist and secular humanist approaches to educating your child. As the saying goes, make the main thing the main thing!

ondary schools spent about 61 percent, and colleges and universities accounted for the remaining 39 percent.[6]

For all of the money that we have spent to educate our children, parents have less confidence today that their children's education is adequate. This increasing lack of confidence started to grow, it could be said, about the time a landmark study by the National Commission on Excellence in Education was released in 1983, comparing U.S. students with their international counterparts. Poignantly, the study was called "A Nation at Risk."

The report gave alarming evidence that America's education system was failing its families. The federal report claimed that American students were "not studying the right subjects, were not working hard enough, and were not learning enough."[7] The report further described the condition of schools as suffering from "slack and uneven standards," and that "many of their teachers were ill-prepared."[8] It also warned that "our social structure would crack, our culture erode, our economy totter, and our national defenses weaken"[9] if the United States did not make immediate attempts to remedy the situation by finding a cure for our fatally ill education system. Some of the sobering descriptions of the failing American system included:

- International comparisons of student achievement on 19 academic tests showed American students were never first or second and, in comparison with other industrialized nations, were last seven times.

- Some 23 million American adults were functionally illiterate by the simplest tests of everyday reading, writing, and comprehension.

- Average achievement of high school students on most standardized tests was lower than 26 years before.
- About 13 percent of all 17-year-olds in the United States were considered functionally illiterate. Functional illiteracy among minority youth ran as high as 40 percent.
- Over half the population of gifted students did not match their tested ability with comparable achievement in school.
- The College Board's Scholastic Aptitude Tests (SATs) demonstrated a virtually unbroken decline from 1963 to 1980. Average verbal scores fell over 50 points and average mathematics scores dropped nearly 40 points.
- Both the number and proportion of students demonstrating superior achievement on the SATs (i.e., those with scores of 650 or higher) had also dramatically declined.[10]

DID YOU KNOW?

For the sake of comparison, consider that elementary and secondary schools and colleges and universities spent an estimated 7.4 percent of the gross domestic product in 2002 to 2003, and that in total, the Department of Education spent 46 percent of the total federal agencies' budget (the Departments of Health and Human Services, Agriculture, Labor, Defense, Interior, and others spent the remainder).[11] Sobering numbers, no doubt, and demonstrative of Americans' commitment to education, just as we saw illustrated in our overview of America's earliest days. The question many Americans have asked, however, is, "What have we gotten for all the dollars we have spent?"

Since these numbers were released over 20 years ago, little has changed academically. But these academic challenges are probably not the greatest ones we face. In today's family, there is evidence that parents have lost their ability to direct their children's education because of the overpowering effect of school culture, peer culture, and the media-driven culture in which we live.

Here's what has occurred in the past 25 years in America's educational system, according to researcher and author Laurence Steinberg. He makes a compelling case that an "extremely high proportion of American high school students do not take school, or their studies, seriously."[12] Over one-third of the students surveyed said that they get through the day in school primarily by "goofing off with their friends," and two-thirds say they cheated on a school test during the past school year.

Overall, Steinberg estimates that about 40 percent of all American students are disengaged from school.[13] In addition, students' time outside of school is "seldom spent in activities that reinforce what they are learning in their classes." Instead, more typically, their time and energy are "focused on activities that compete with, rather then complement, their studies." Adolescent peer culture continues to be the most defining influence in a young person's life.

Scene 6: A View from High Ground: Education and the Take-Charge Parent

The sweeping No Child Left Behind legislation (NCLB) in 2001 has not proved a panacea for our country's education woes, but it has introduced a powerful notion: *accountability.* For the first time, moms and dads whose children attend neighborhood public schools have recourse if their children attend a school that scores "needs improvement," the euphemism among educators for "failing." Now if a

A Profile of Education in America Today[14]

Our Public Schools Today

- 47.6 million students
- 94,112 schools
- Of these, 3,400 are charter schools
- $500 billion spent on K-12 public schools, 42.7 percent of which is raised from local taxes, 49 percent from state taxes, and 8.4 percent from federal taxes
- Average per pupil expenditure—$8,019
- Highest—District of Columbia at $13,328
- Lowest—Utah at $4,860

Our Private Schools Today

- 5.9 million students
- 27,223 schools
- Average tuition, elementary schools—less than $3,500
- Average tuition, secondary schools—$6,052

Fourth Grade Achievement, as measured in public school tests

- 31 percent proficient in reading
- 32 percent proficient in mathematics
- 29 percent proficient in science

school cannot demonstrate improvement, tutoring services become available to students, school choice options kick in, and eventually the school risks being taken over by the state education system and even shut down.

- 18 percent proficient in American history
- Half as many poor students were proficient in these subjects

Graduation Rates

- 71 percent of public school students graduate on time
- 24 percent of Americans have a bachelor's or higher degree

International Comparison

- U.S. eighth graders ranked 12th out of 45 countries in math and 8th in science
- U.S. 12th graders ranked 18th out of 21 countries in combined math and science literacy scores

School Choice

- Vouchers—7 states and Washington, D.C.
- Tax credits—6 states
- Charter school laws—40 states and Washington, D.C.

Homeschooling

- 50 states and Washington, D.C.
- As many as 2 million students are homeschooled nationwide
- Gives parents the freedom to choose the curriculum that best meets their children's needs
- Creates diverse learning environments
- Promotes satisfaction and academic improvement

Are these changes resulting in vast improvements in the American landscape of education? No. But what might be occurring are profound changes in the *expectations* parents have for their child's education. Though NCLB is by no means perfect legislation, it introduced key ingredients to long-term change: *accountability* and *choice*. I expect we will see that in retrospect, accountability and choice will have initiated a new movement among take-charge parents.

As a result, there are bright and encouraging signs today, includ-

---

Education in Early America and Now:
Books and Homework[15]

Then: Books brought to and from school (if any; often families could not afford books) were bound by a leather strip and carried on the hip. Students did very little homework because of the demands of the agricultural life and the need of children's work contribution at home.

Now: Students stuff backpacks with many books, some today pulling them behind them on wheels because of the weight of the pack. Students are expected to spend sometimes hours after school and on weekends doing homework because it is seen as a vital component of a comprehensive education.

The Classroom

Then: Children sat on three-legged stools or on pine or oak benches behind long and narrow tables, which were often handmade by the parents of the schoolchildren. Eventually, children sat at individual desks that were bolted to the floor, boys on one side of the room and girls on the other. Younger children sat at the front of the room, closest to the teacher.

ing the growth of the charter school movement within the public school system, establishment of the homeschool movement as a powerful education option, the increase in attendance at conservative Christian schools, and variations on the voucher options. Each of these options has relative strengths and weaknesses, and a couple of them have generated controversy, but what we do see in each of these education options is the opportunity for parents to engage the education process. We call these parents *take-charge parents.*

Now: After small, round tables were introduced in the 1960s, teachers started to move around the classroom, encouraging students to work collaboratively, relying on each other's knowledge and skills. In this setting, the teacher's role is that of a learning facilitator. Today, both individual portable desks and round tables are found in schools across America.

Testing

Then: Tests and quizzes were common in nineteenth-century schools. Usually, they were given through an oral stand-up quiz at the end of the school day. The first major standardized test was introduced in the 1870s, an entrance exam given to high school students that required two days of testing.

Now: A wide variety of testing forms are used in American classrooms today, including short, informal quizzes and tests, standardized tests like the California Achievement Tests, the SAT, the Iowa Test of Basic Skills, as well as numerous state-specific tests. The goal of course is for educators to measure aptitude, critical thinking skills, and content-area knowledge. Recent education changes have increased pressure for schools to be accountable, placing more attention on testing and accountability.

The challenge before us today is how we help both parents and their children in the education process, for if we are successful there, then we will be on our way to solving one of the largest issues that moms and dads face today—how to provide their children with the training they need in order to be all that God intends them to be in their world.

DID YOU KNOW?

Following WW II, the G.I. Bill (officially known at the Servicemen's Readjustment Act of 1944) provided a college education for veterans. In the seven years following the war, over two million people began attending college, more than doubling the population. Because the law provides the same opportunity for every veteran (regardless of background, class, or race), the long-standing tradition that college is for the wealthy was effectively broken.

3

The Take-Charge Parent

by Marc Fey

Education is not a form of entertainment, but a means of empowering people to take control of their lives.

—UNKNOWN

In a multitude of counselors there is safety.

—PROVERBS 24:6 (NKJV)

"Do you understand what you are reading?"
Philip asked. "How can I,"
[the Ethiopian ruler] said,
"unless someone explains it to me?"

—ACTS 8:30-31

The famous author C. S. Lewis eloquently described the role of parenting this way: "We feed children in order that they may soon be able to feed themselves; we teach them in order that they may soon not need our teaching."[1] Lewis calls this "Gift-love," which is to say that the goal of the parent is not "what I give" but rather "what my child learns to give." Take-charge parents keep this ultimate outcome front and center in all they do to raise their children toward adulthood.

How each parent accomplishes this outcome is as varied as the circumstances we face, but the take-charge attitudes will be similar, as you will see in the scenarios that follow.

Roger was receiving a great education at a high school prep school. But after his family moved to a new city, his parents discovered there were no options similar to the kind of education Roger had received. So when Elsa and Paul learned of the academically rigorous International Baccalaureate program in town, they made sure they purchased a house in the right school district. For this family, the program was a great fit and provided a rigorous academic challenge.

Cheryl and Bruce had always homeschooled their seven children. As their oldest, Daniel, reached high school showing great ability in academics, music, and athletics, they considered enrolling him in the local high school. Through the process of finding out about the program, they also deliberated enrolling three more of their children, too. In the end, they decided to stay the course with homeschooling, and instead signed up Daniel as an off-campus homeschool student in the fall soccer program where he was able to better develop his athletic talents.

• • •

Melinda and Andy's three daughters attended a private Christian school—at a cost. Melinda maintained a thriving physical therapy business and also was working on her doctorate; Andy had a successful accounting practice. This combination of responsibilities made driving the girls to and from school a challenge, as was the significant tuition price. Melinda and Andy managed to find a way with some carpooling help from Grandpa, and at the end of the day, the strong spiritual and academic education made the sacrifices worth it.

All of these parents illustrate what it means to be a *take-charge parent*. Each of the solutions is different, but each choice was made by parents who were clearly in charge of their children's education.

In just half a generation, the three scenarios above have become commonplace. For example, in the past 20 years, the homeschool movement has established itself as an option, with an estimated 1.6 to 2.0 million children today being taught at home by their parents.[2] This is a phenomenal development, and now of course a mainstream and well-respected option for parents. Similarly, though the charter school movement started a relatively short time ago with the St. Paul Academy in Minnesota in 1993, today there are over 4,000 schools in operation, representing unprecedented change in an institution typically brittle to reform. Also, Christian schools have grown from an estimated 2,500 in 1972 to over 9,000 schools today, comprising more than 25 percent of all private schools in the country. Things have changed indeed.

However, the options have come because of the crisis facing our schools and families, and that crisis has only increased in recent years. In fact, you and I face tremendous challenges as parents today because of three specific conditions in the education environment. First, nearly one-third of parents are completely "out of the loop" in their child's education.[3] Parental disengagement explains why about 84 percent of students report that their parents don't care what grades they receive, and serves as a predictor of student behavior problems like alcohol and drug abuse, delinquency and violence, sexual promiscuity, and not surprisingly, low academic achievement and learning difficulties.[4]

Second, today's peer culture often demeans student academic achievement and puts down students who try to be successful in school.[5] Fewer than one in five students say their friends consider it important to get good grades.[6] Even in many Christian schools, negative student peer pressure toward academic success creates dissonance for students who work to be successful. In fact, there are indications that Christian school students are in many ways not very different from their public school counterparts. One study noted that 68 percent of public school students reported cheating on a test in the past year, while 70 percent of Christian school students had.

In my own teaching experience in a California public high school, I found the student culture and the school's authority on campus to be constantly at odds. The energy that it took to teach *and* address this negative culture complicated the learning process, to say the least.

Parents face a third challenge: the busyness and speed of today's life. The Mach 5 pace of parents and kids leaves little room for the kinds of activities that foster academic achievement. From various after-school activities and two-parent working household schedules, to a dense, media-driven environment including TV, video games, and iPods, kids' schedules today leave little time for activities that would complement classroom learning.

As a result, you and I must have a clear vision of what kind of parent it will take to navigate the rough waters of educating our children. That is what the rest of this chapter is about—discussing and describing what a *take-charge parent* is.

A take-charge parent thinks ahead about decisions that need to be made and how they will be made. The word "proactive" describes one who "acts before a situation becomes a source of confrontation or crisis" and acts within a situation by "causing something to happen rather than waiting to respond to it after it happens." If ever there was a time when parents need to be proactive, it is today. So, for the rest of this chapter, we will explore what it means to be a take-charge parent. Specifically, we will discuss—

The take-charge parent as *CONSUMER.*

The take-charge parent as *CRITICAL DECISION-MAKER.*

The take-charge parent as *COACH.*

The take-charge parent as *COLLABORATOR.*

The take-charge parent as *CHAMPION.*

The first two, Consumer and Critical Decision-Maker, describe your relationship with the school or other setting where your child learns. The third role, Coach, describes your relationship with your child. The fourth and fifth roles, Collaborator and Champion, describe your relationship with your child, the school or other learning setting, and the community of students and parents that makes up that learning environment. Let's discuss these roles one at a time.

Parent as Consumer

As a consumer of education products, your opinion counts. At least it should. And the more you and I understand the power we wield as consumers, the greater will be the options that are provided to us. Those options will include better homeschool curriculum and products, better trained teachers and education leaders, and more varied school options.

Education in America is a lot of things, but one thing is clear—it is big money. The economics of education is the backdrop for high-stakes battles over education ideas, and you only have to look at the great lengths that the National Education Association goes to protecting its monopoly on public schools to see how high the stakes are— just "follow the money," as the saying goes.

The trend to provide parents like you and me with options requires a reappropriation of tax dollars, which explains why new options like charter schools are so threatening to the public education establishment. When your son or daughter moves to a charter school, for example, the money the local school district receives for educating your child is moved to the charter school.

What these simple examples illustrate is that you and I are consumers of the services that our schools are providing. In particular,
public schools are more motivated today to provide services to parents and children. Slowly, they are beginning to understand that their
very future depends on their ability to meet the specific needs voiced
by parents. Change is slow, but in many communities it is happening. Whether or not the increasingly secular curriculum and education philosophy are too much to overcome is for each parent to
determine. Certainly, the options available in each community need
to be evaluated. Your job as a consumer of education resources requires
that you be a smart and well-informed consumer.

Of course Christian schools and other private schools already
understand that they are service providers because it is not the government writing the monthly check to educate the children they serve.
In most cases they are very aware that parents are writing the check,
so accountability goes up. If parents are not satisfied, they stop writing checks. In the case of public education, unfortunately, the government doesn't stop writing checks even if the services being provided
are subpar. This is the reason you and I must step into our rightful
place as consumers of education and exercise one of our most important powers—choice.

Here are recommendations for developing a consumer approach
to your child's education:

Investigate the options in your area. Depending on your education philosophy, start with the local neighborhood schools. Ask questions about specific programs and academic tracks. Then move to
investigating charter schools, magnet schools, Christian schools and

other private schools, and homeschool associations. For example, in my family's area, there is a virtual homeschool charter school that provides a computer, Internet connection, curriculum, and teacher support, all delivered to your home. Unless you do your homework, you may be unaware of all the options available to you.

Know the economics of providing an education for your child. What does homeschooling cost? What do the private schools cost? What are all the costs, including time and money, of attending a charter school (since transportation and some other costs are common among charter school programs)?

Be sure to approach the providers of your child's education as a consumer. In other words, expect good service, adequate information, and respect as a consumer of the education goods and services being provided. This frame of mind will do a lot in helping you to proactively engage the key people involved in your child's education.

Expect results. There needs to be a good return on the money, time, and energy that is being spent to provide your child's education. Track annual test scores of your child and your child's school and district, watch the emotional health of your child, and look into the relative national and state rankings for your child's school district. Also, measure results based on the worldview that your child is receiving at his or her place of education. At worst, the education option you choose should not be damaging to your child's faith. If it is negative and actually goes against the Christian worldview and values you are teaching in the home, be prepared to look for a new option.

Develop a core team of education experts, friends, and acquaintances who seem to have the "inside track" on education issues or who have good common sense and practical wisdom. Stay in touch, ask a lot of questions, and keep on the learning curve as an educated consumer.

Parent as Critical Decision-Maker

As a take-charge parent, you are the critical decision-maker in your child's education. Once you have researched your options and have initiated relationships with key individuals and groups in your child's education, you are prepared to make the important decisions for what is best for your child.

To become an effective critical decision-maker, you must have a consistent approach on which to base your decisions. Take-charge parents are consistent without being rigid, and the difference is that consistency is adapted to fit the situation, whereas rigidness applies the same decision regardless of the situation. Decide early what is going to drive your decisions, then stay with that until it stops working.

Earlier, we discussed the idea of non-negotiables. These are especially important in being a critical decision-maker because there will be some situations that require you to take decisive action. Perhaps you notice a shift in your child's attitude toward school, you are not satisfied with the academic challenge of your child's school, or you find the school is unable to control the bullying that your child and others are dealing with.

In one example, a single mother's first-grade daughter attended a public charter school that was not providing the reading instruction that the mother felt was necessary. The mother worked hard to resolve the situation, but eventually, when she found the teacher and principal defensive and hard to work with, she realized that a change was in order. The non-negotiable was the strongly held belief that she needed to have a partnering relationship, not an adversarial relationship, with her child's teacher and school. Though it was midyear, she made the hard but courageous decision to move her child to a nearby private Christian school.

Here are some recommendations for developing an approach to critical decision-making in your child's education:

Set goals and analyze the results. Sometimes you evaluate results in an informal way—perhaps you follow the hunch that your child's peer group is pulling her down, not building her up. Other times, the statistics you find on your child's school may provide you with information that helps you make the right decision.

Scan the landscape of options, listen for the stories of what is happening in your local area, then be sure that you are making key decisions in your child's best interests. Depending on how your child is doing, this can be an annual process.

As a critical decision-maker, strive to be a problem-solver, not just a decision-maker. Where it is possible, use your decisions to solve problems and promote a collaborative approach with parents, teachers, school staff, and education experts. We will talk more about this in the "parent as collaborator" section.

Keep your list of non-negotiables short. You will want to base most of your decisions on wisdom specific to the situation, since decisions based on non-negotiables are the exception, not the rule, with decision-making. The key? Stay flexible and creative with the challenges you are facing.

Communicate these non-negotiables clearly to your child (in language appropriate for him or her). Also, consider different scenarios that might require you to act on your non-negotiables. Take time as parents to discuss these scenarios; it's especially important that you present a united front when making a decision.

Parent as Coach

As a take-charge parent, you are your child's most important education coach. Your coaching makes a difference in your child's life, first through your example and later through your leadership in your child's education experience.

Children learn first by watching. The first thing your child is paying attention to is your attitude toward learning. You probably had your own set of challenges and setbacks. Maybe you struggled to get good grades. Maybe you earned straight A's. All of your own school and learning experiences have shaped your attitudes toward education, and those beliefs and attitudes will undoubtedly influence how you coach your child. If you are a perfectionist in your education approach, your child will internalize this. If you demonstrate a negative attitude toward teachers in general, your child will most likely adopt your attitude.

Remember that you are on stage all the time, and for better or for worse, your child will take his or her cues from you. Your child will pay close attention to the way you handle your own mistakes and failures. One of the key qualities I have observed in successful and well-adjusted students is a confidence and willingness to take risks and make mistakes. Invariably, parents who don't allow room for children to make mistakes create a kind of stress around the learning process that is hard for the children to overcome.

Your coaching should also include meaningful time together "on task" and "off task." Many parents don't realize that their investment in quality time together, apart from school tasks and responsibilities, actually improves the quality of a child's time spent on homework and class assignments. When mom and dad build into their schedule meaningful quality time—and this is not to be confused with lots of activities—the child is often more successful with schoolwork.

Practical coaching also includes adapting to where your child is developmentally. As your son or daughter grows and matures, your parenting must also change and adapt. Also, the older your child is, the more important is your understanding of his or her temperament and learning style. There are numerous resources, many identified later in this book, to help you adapt your coaching approach to your child's temperament and developmental needs.

Finally, communication is your primary tool as the coach. Great sports coaches are tremendous communicators. No one style is the best. However, all great coaches find powerful ways to connect with their players. Your communication style and the content of what you say are very important. Simple yet key components of good communication include: (1) hearing your child's point of view, (2) having real dialogue, (3) setting up regular times for good communication,

(4) protecting your conversations about your child's education from escalated levels of anger or negative emotion, and (5) making good communication a common goal of the family in all relationships.

Below are recommendations for developing a "coach" approach to your child's education:

Share your own education and learning experiences, both the positive and negative (in age-appropriate ways). Your child will benefit greatly from your direction and advice if she or he understands your own experience and the "why" of the advice that you are giving.

Monitor your child's development. There are a number of great resources on child development, and the areas that you will want to monitor are emotional and psychological, academic, physical, and spiritual. Understand that the education setting will contribute significantly to your child's development in each of these areas. Study the ways they all relate together, supporting or hindering progress and development.

Investigate your child's temperament and learning style preferences. Focus on the Family has excellent resources to help you in your investigation. Also, you can find many resources in the education section of your library or local bookstore. Share this new information with his or her teachers and with your child. Build ongoing discussion and problem-solving approaches around this important information.

Emphasize your relationship with your child over your child's academic performance. As a good coach does, affirm consistently and often that *who* your child is is more important than what kinds of grades he or she gets. Work very hard not to let your academic for example coaching ("Did you do your homework?") get in the way of your relationship, but rather use it to strengthen your relationship as you learn to work together to solve the educational challenges that will inevitably arise.

Continually work on keeping your communication positive and hopeful. This is often a matter of carving out the time to have the encouraging talks, not just waiting until there is a problem to discuss academics. Structure a time every week or every month to sit down with the same three or four questions, such as: "What is one thing that is making you a better student?" "What is one thing that is helping you to be successful?" "Is there anything that you need to tell me about your school experience, either positive or negative?" and, "Do you know that I care more about who you are than the grades you get?"

Parent as Collaborator

The take-charge parent will assemble a support team for educating his/her child. Depending on your school option (even homeschool), your team will include other parents, teachers, school staff, or education experts. Not only should you not try to educate your child on your own, it might be nearly impossible to do so.

Collaborating with Other Parents

Collaborating with other parents is very valuable toward making sure that your child is receiving the best education possible. Here is why. The peer culture in the teen years is by far the most formative influence in your child's life. Some parents refuse to give in to this, trying to overwhelm this peer influence with family time and extra church services and youth-group activities, for example. However, what the research tells us is that it is your ability to choose your child's friends, not your attempts to neutralize their influence, that determines most directly your child's likely success in school. To the extent you can pick your kid's friends, you are down the road to achieving your objectives as a parent.

And obviously, the best way to choose the right peer group for your child is to get to know his or her friends' parents. Probably the most important factor in our satisfaction with our children's education is that we have become close friends with our children's friends. We know what their families stand for. We know what they teach. We know what their expectations are. And because of that, we provide a united front with all of our kids. Over time, as I continue to get to know my children's friends, I can also be a positive influence in their lives.

Take the time to invest in solid relationships with the parents of your child's friends. For example, we dads have taken our boys camping for the weekend, as couples we are in a Bible study together, and more than a few holidays like Christmas and Thanksgiving have been spent with the families of our kids' friends. In a sense, what we are creating is a small town in our big suburban community.

Collaborating with Teachers and School Staff
Collaborating with teachers and school staff is more than volunteering in the classroom. It's more than bringing this week's snack. And it

is far more than showing up at back-to-school night. In fact, if you ask educators, collaboration involves helping your child with homework, communicating with teachers, collaborating with the education community, and volunteering in the many opportunities provided in the education setting. Still, it is far more than that. True collaboration works when we forge alliances around agreed-upon goals.

Many school leaders are recognizing the powerful influence of parents as collaborators, particularly among the most challenging communities. One principal, Cheryl Shrewsbury of Turnbull Learning Academy in San Mateo, California, described her school's relationship with parents, noting that "they can feel intimidated, but when parents participate in the school, we get tremendous results because parents realize they have something to offer."[7]

To build collaborative relationships with educators, develop a team approach. First, spend the time getting to know your child's teachers. Expect teachers to communicate clearly and often, and do your part proactively to communicate your expectations, family activities, and insights about your child. Also consider offering your expertise in the classroom—professional or personal. Finally, consider celebrating your child's successes with your child's teacher and school staff.

Collaborating with Education Experts

Today collaboration with education experts occurs through books, seminars, and online resources. But it can also happen as you identify the influential people in your community (church, local neighborhood, and town) and build intentional relationships with them. One mother began a once-a-month informal gathering at a local coffe house, where they tackled one education "big idea" and one education "practical strategy" at each meeting. The group consisted of parents and a core of education experts, including former teachers, a retired Christian school administrator, and a tutor, each sharing ideas, helping to solve problems, and offering encouragement to one another.

Parent as Champion

One definition of a champion is "an ardent supporter of another person."[8] That clearly describes your role as parent and educator in your child's life. To champion your child's long-term success throughout his or her education experience, you will need to have the larger story in clear focus, an indefatigable commitment to overcome obstacles, and a realistic view of your child's strengths and weaknesses. And finally, you will be successful if you can achieve all of this from within the education solution you choose for your child.

One of the most important gifts that we can give to our children is the glimpse of the larger, transcendent story of eternity, which is being worked out in the day-to-day events of our lives. The famous British poet and priest Gerard Manley Hopkins described God's larger story this way: "It is not only prayer that gives God glory but work: smiting on an anvil, sawing a beam, whitewashing a wall, driving horses, sweeping, scouring, everything gives God glory if being in his grace you do it as your duty."[9] Add together all the activities that make up your child's day at school, and you have the spirit of Hopkins' statement applied to your child's education. Our important job is to help our children to look up and see God's story being worked out in the day-to-day events of school. A tall order, no doubt, but so important.

Your indefatigable commitment to overcome obstacles models for your child what will become his or her own most important skill of all—the ability to persevere. Most achievements in school occur because of one key character trait—the ability to persevere through difficult circumstances. The mistake that we often make is to require perseverance from our children but overlook the importance of actually building it into their lives one challenge at a time. The fact is, we first build perseverance into our children's lives through modeling. Then from our example we can teach our children about the building blocks of perseverance, which include discipline, hard work, and the power of an optimistic, hopeful attitude toward difficult tasks.

Finally, championing your child's success in school occurs through a realistic appraisal of your child's strengths and weaknesses. In my years as a teacher, one of the toughest situations I faced was in dealing with parents who would not accept the input of teachers, test scores, and other descriptions of their child's strengths and weaknesses. Parents typically erred in one of two ways. Either they had an inflated view of their child's strengths, or they had an unhealthy focus on their child's weaknesses. To strike a balance is the goal. Even when grades or test scores paint a gray picture, it is important to affirm your child's skills and abilities. And likewise, even when straight A's are being earned, it is important to have a sober view of blind spots and weaknesses.

Here are recommendations for championing your child's success in education:

Celebrate goals and milestones that you and your child reach. Some parents keep a journal to remember the successes, others reward milestones through special dinners or added privileges. Jotting down the milestone should take only five minutes in many cases, and it will help you to set aside time every month to celebrate your child's progress and accomplishments. Whatever your approach, be sure to set reachable and measurable goals, and then celebrate success, small and big.

Champion your child's success by setting a context for school. Help your child to understand that school can be more than just boring, or the place where he or she meets with friends. Be sure to think through the language you will use to describe what school is all about—a place where we learn the skills to grow and develop throughout life, a place where we develop our skills to be a good worker, and most importantly, a place where we learn to practice and live out the truths of the Bible—for example, truths like "be faithful with a little and you will be faithful with much."

Cheer on your child, especially when the going is tough. Slow down and notice the daily ups and downs of your child's education experience. If you carve out the time for the smaller ups and downs, the ones that occur day-to-day, then you are a lot less likely to miss the big ones. And, you will have the communication patterns in place with your child to work through the hard times when they come.

Be a positive influence in your child's life and in the education community by being winsome in your approach and optimistic in your disposition. Watch what you say about your child's teachers and school. Confine your criticism to discussions with your spouse and with other adults who are helping you to work toward a solution. More students' attitudes are tainted by their own parents' negative attitudes than you might imagine. Believe the best, choosing a winsome approach in your dealings with educators and other parents.

Be clear about the goal. Yes, skills are important. Knowledge is critical. But at the end of the day, your child's spiritual and character development is the real payoff of a good education. Help your child to connect activities in the classroom—reading, writing, computing, completing assignments, taking tests—to what is developed on the inside through these activities. Again, *it is about who your child is becoming, not just what he or she is doing.*

How to Create Success in Today's Educational Environment

by Jim Mhoon

Education commences at the mother's knee,
and every word spoken within the hearing of little
children tends toward the formation of character.
—HOSEA BALLOU

So we fix our eyes not on what is seen, but on what is unseen.
For what is seen is temporary, but what is unseen is eternal.
—2 CORINTHIANS 4:18

The streets of Istanbul are crowded with more than just people. Vendors offering "the best deal" call to passersby, their voices blending with engine noise, music, and the buzz from the crowd. Smoke rises from makeshift grills—the smells of charring meats, vegetables, spices, and herbs mix with auto exhaust, tobacco smoke, and rotting garbage. The colorful displays of carpets, drums, handmade shoes, and trinkets make your eyes hurt. It is a little difficult to keep your bearings when first encountering this environment because it's a sensory overload.

In that overstimulating environment, something unusual happened. I stopped in the midst of chaos and ordered ice cream from a street vendor. I had two choices: chocolate or vanilla. It came on a cone. That was it. I chose vanilla.

There is something gratifying about making a simple choice, especially in a world where simple choices are increasingly rare. Have you taken your family out for ice cream recently? How about for coffee? It used to be a simple matter of ordering decaf or regular. Now we're required to learn a second language. We are expected to know the difference between a tall, grande, and venti. We can order a café au lait, latte, or cappuccino; iced coffee, Peruvian blend, or café con leche; and espresso crème, espresso macchiato, or espresso medici. Our culture has demanded choices, and we have learned to navigate within the result.

School choice is not exactly a new idea. The truth is that most of us grew up in a traditional education system and attended the school selected for us by the local district's boundaries. Common practice was to default to the neighborhood school, and few families took the matter much further. The only other alternative for most families was a private school, most commonly associated with a church or parish.

Even in such a limited education environment, parents still exercised choice, mostly in the form of choosing to live in a region with a preferred school. For generations families have elected to purchase homes based upon proximity to a well-reputed school. As circumstances permit, good parents will make an effort to do what's best for their children's education success.

That hasn't changed, but education options have. Today, education options abound, and that's good news. The bad news is that parents face a bewildering array of options, and the best choice is rarely obvious. As with the ice cream store that offers 40 flavors, 12 varieties of cones and cups, and dozens of mix-ins, it is often a matter of personal preference. Even so, this choice is an important one, and wise parents pay careful attention to the needs of their children and their family and seek to provide the most successful education they can garner.

Certain important principles apply to selecting the best education environment for your children, regardless of what your options are. Here are some guidelines to consider as you select a school for your child.

PRINCIPLE 1:
Seeking utopia is a fool's errand.

The perfect education system does not exist. Period. There are simply too many variables. They range from the interests and personalities of students to the state of the facilities, qualifications of the instructors, quality of the curriculum, family priorities, cultural settings—you get the idea. Your task is not to find the perfect setting; rather, it is to find the setting that serves your child and family the best and then find ways to take advantage of the strengths and mitigate the weaknesses.

It's all about the results. In some small communities there are few choices; however, the likelihood of having personal relationships with teachers and administrators is much higher. In such a setting, the community is intimately involved in the school. As a result, you have more influence within that single choice than those who live in an urban environment where people are less connected and community is difficult to develop.

Principle 2:
Understanding the point of education is vital.

Acquiring a high-quality education for our children can become a pursuit similar to idol worship. Americans in our culture often bow down to academic achievement, college placement, career advancement, social status, and financial reward. Christian parents must put all of these things in perspective. On one hand, we want strong Christian young people to achieve critical positions in the marketplace, but it will do little good for the kingdom if they acquire position but spend their influence pursuing wealth and status.

In the book *Home Court Advantage*, Dr. Kevin Leman challenges parents to get to the real point of education, which is to build character.

> Your son may be able to recite the value for pi to the tenth digit, but how fairly does he divide his candy with his siblings? Your daughter may be a cheerleader, homecoming queen, or valedictorian—but how well does she treat the "anonymous" girls who walk invisibly down the halls at school?[1]

We must emphasize those things that really matter—the "unseen," eternal values of love and the Christian faith.

Principle 3:
The choice you make is less important than the role you play.

Significant long-term research confirms the importance of parents and family to academic success. Whether we're exploring character education or success in math, research points to one thing: The home environment is the very best indicator of academic success. Note that it's not the school facility, the neighborhood where you reside, the teacher or her education, or the money spent per student. All else pales in significance if a child has parents who value education, involve themselves in education, and provide a home environment conducive to learning. Your involvement is *the* key to your child's academic success.

PRINCIPLE 4:
School choice does matter, but perhaps not for the reason you think.

Your involvement and family circumstances are the most important variables in predicting academic success. The same applies for all families. Yes, different schools do have different approaches to education, and those approaches do make a difference. Matching the philosophy of education to your child's learning style, interests, and your family values are all-important aspects of choosing a school. Even so, one of the most important aspects of school choice has to do with peers. Research and experience tell us that parents are the primary influencers of their children, especially in the early years. According to research done by Dr. Lawrence Steinberg of Temple University, as children begin to enter adolescence, however, parental influence begins to lose ground to the influence of peer groups. In fact, peer groups become a major factor influencing academic success in high school.[2]

The message is clear: If you want your child to succeed academically, get involved personally and surround your children with peers who have parents like you—involved, principled, and insistent on academic achievement.

Our family has been blessed with such environments for our daughter. She enrolled in a school-within-a-school where the students had to apply to the rigorous high school program—the application process ensures that the students want to be there. That program attracts motivated families who are willing to do what it takes to excel in school. The result is a peer group of *families* that share a common goal, families that demand excellence, students who are engaged, events that are full of supporters, and teachers who compete to teach in the program.

Keys to Education Success

In an article titled "If Families Matter Most, Where Do Schools Come In?" Harvard economist Dr. Caroline Hoxby explores the most important variables predicting academic success. She compares school variables, neighborhood variables, and family variables as they apply to success in math. The results of her study are stunning: Predicting

Rules of Thumb for Selecting Successful Schools

Remember that your parental involvement is more important than anything the school can provide. As such, there is a natural "rising tide" when you engage in a school that serves families like yours.

Curriculum varies widely by school. Don't be afraid of advanced and challenging coursework; the average motivated student can excel in these environments. The greater danger is placement in a program that utilizes inferior academics or plays to the lowest common denominator instead of challenging students to stretch their abilities.

Check with the school's principal and grade-level teachers to get an understanding of their philosophy of education. Key ideas include parent involvement, academic standards, high standing in standardized tests, a belief that all students can excel, emphasis on safety, and zero tolerance policies pertaining to substance use and violent behavior.

academic success has very little to do with the neighborhood (3 percent of the variance) or the school (4 percent) and has almost everything to do with the family (93 percent). Dr. Hoxby put it this way: "Family inputs account for success anywhere between 11 and 14 times both neighborhood and school variables combined."[3]

Other economists, however, point out that variables such as number of books in the home, ownership of a computer, or the presence of a dictionary or atlas (all variables in Hoxby's analysis) do not provide any academic "magic." Rather, they are evidence of a family where academic excellence precedes the child. In other words, those resources exist in the home because the parents themselves are educated, and they read books and use reference tools. You can't just drop off an atlas and books at someone's door and expect the child to succeed academically.

Parental Success Breeds Future Success

When thinking about developing a legacy for coming generations, it is helpful to bear this in mind: Providing your child with the best education within your means will benefit them, but it will also benefit future generations. The key is intentionality and perseverance now for the sake of the future. If you believe that each generation builds upon prior generations (see Deuteronomy 4), you can begin to take action now on behalf of your children, grandchildren, and great-grandchildren by getting personally involved in education. There is a positive correlation between the education level of mothers and the academic opportunity and success ratios of children.[4]

Simply put, your success leads to the success of your children. And since you are reading this book, you are likely already doing a great job as it relates to your child's academic success. Sadly, many parents who need this book the most won't use it. But you can take the opportunity to effect change in the community from your own sphere of influence.

Selectivity Most Often Yields Success

A debate rages regarding schools that require students to academically qualify for their program. Many administrators and educators believe that such programs unfairly limit the ability of students who could achieve if given the chance and prefer to provide programs with open enrollment standards so long as the student maintains minimum grade standards. As a parent, you like selectivity. If your child qualifies for a program that you believe in, don't worry too much about the social ramifications. Do what is best for your children. There will be plenty of challenges for them later. If your child doesn't qualify, look for other programs or activities that offer a high commitment level and a challenge.

Our daughter has had experience in both settings. She did equally well in a test-in program and an open-enrollment environment. Now she is in a private school setting and still achieving academically. Our experience in all three programs has led me to conclude that the program itself is less important than the individual student, the opportunity to be challenged, and a peer group that draws the very best out of the child and family.

Spiritual Success Comes from Good Parenting

Here's an additional point to ponder. If family variables are so overwhelming as they relate to success in school, what effect do you think they have on matters of the spirit? No matter which schooling option you choose for your child, spiritual values need to be nurtured through the family, and if good values are taught in school, teachers and administrators need your help to support those programs and reinforce those concepts at home.

As a specialist in family issues, I communicate with family ministers, educators, coaches, and others who work with families and children. One of the common complaints I hear pertains to the level of involvement of parents in the lives of their children. Many feel that parents have handed them the responsibility to "own" certain parts of raising children. The problem is that people who love children and want the best for them often allow roles to blur and fall into the trap of taking on parental responsibility that is beyond their capability. This is a problem because even the best attempts will fail, since no one can replace a mom and dad. Ask yourself these questions:

- Who is the primary spiritual trainer of your child? Is it you or the youth pastor?
- Who taught your son about sex? You or the school?
- Does your church or school run programs that seem inappropriate to you? Have you explored why?

I coach ministers and educators on finding ways to get parents more involved. I believe so strongly in parental involvement that I often encourage them to drop some programs in order to force the issue. "Don't take that role from parents," I say. "Find ways to help them fulfill it." In response, I hear the same lament over and over: "If we don't do it, the parents won't either."

As a program developer, I can tell you that it is difficult to get a response from today's busy families. The company I work for conducts research on the needs and wants of parents and then creates programs

---

How Much Does Parent Involvement Matter?

Parent involvement is

- holding your child accountable to achieve good grades
- providing a home environment conducive to learning—a quiet location for studying, a peaceful environment, and resources such as a dictionary, atlas, computer, etc.
- knowing your child's teachers
- knowing the classroom learning objectives for the year
- assisting your student with difficult problems or challenging assignments
- attending school events

Parent involvement is not

- doing assignments for your student
- obsessing over your student being the best reader in the class
- insisting that everyone around you acknowledge your child's exceptional talents
- chastising the teacher for holding your child accountable for behavior, quality of work, timeliness, etc.
- expecting your child to be treated as a special case (unless your child has a special need)

meant to meet those very needs, but the response rate is usually disappointing. In fact, I've spoken to high-profile church leaders who consider 10 percent participation in a spiritual training program for church families to be as good as they can expect. With that sort of response, it is often tempting for them to simply bypass the family and go directly to the child; after all, they have them captive in Sunday school, sports leagues, and the classroom.

You will encounter many well-meaning "helpers" in your tenure as a parent. They will offer your child teaching or resources that will be well done, accurate, and even godly. Nevertheless, you must not hand the responsibility off to someone else. There is simply too much at stake. Furthermore, there is a biblical model that is God's revelation to parents about how our children are wired to learn. Deuteronomy 4 and 6 both refer to teaching the laws of God to our children. Those scriptures are speaking to parents, and they reveal God's design for such matters. The laws of God are meant to be passed from *parent to child*, and there is something supernatural and spiritual in that transaction. Sure, let someone else teach math if you must, but don't give up matters of the spirit. Teach them personally and reap the benefits of God's design.

Success in a Changing World

One day a mother pulled me aside to talk about her family circumstance. She attended a church where homeschooling was becoming the norm. She and I agreed that we thought it was a good thing to see, but she had a secret: "I don't think I want to homeschool my son!

What should I do?" In a world that was once dominated by the public school establishment, I found her question ironic.

Choosing a successful school program for your child is an important task. All parents want their children to be in a safe, nurturing environment. They want their children to learn, to express excitement about the world they are discovering, and to gain important skills for their future. Today, the opportunity to achieve that goal is very real. While there is still a great need for reform, we have many well-prepared teachers, more homeschool programs to choose from, and greater access to information and help.

Yet we can feel overwhelmed as we sort through the options and information. We are bombarded with news about the failing public school system, but we know public school teachers who are great professionals. We read articles from concerned experts who doubt the validity of homeschooling, but we know homeschool families who are raising exceptional children. We hear ads from private schools that tout academic achievement and college placement, but we can't seem to find a way to afford tuition. Our family and friends are ready to advise us and urge us to adopt the program they have selected for their children.

So where do we start? Set aside all the global statistics, advice, conflicting data, and peer pressure and realize that your child is an individual who has specific talents and abilities. Look at your options, prayerfully consider them, weed out those that are not realistic, and make a decision with confidence that you have the ability to make it successful.

But don't stop there! Continually improve your circumstance, making changes when they are appropriate, involving yourself as much as possible and creating a network and community of friends and advocates who are facing the same struggles you face. You'll find that a successful school experience for your children is within your grasp.

Plan Ahead for Change

Begin early and plan ahead for change. After your fall parent-teacher conferences or three months of homeschooling, you should have enough information about your child's education success (or lack thereof) to know if you want to continue or explore other options. By January, it would be wise to have a plan and begin submitting applications to private schools and/or for district transfers. If you are looking into homeschooling, you'll need to select curriculum or apply to virtual academies. Some private schools have long waiting lists. If you're in doubt about a certain school, apply anyway. You can always turn down the seat if you choose a different option. See chapter 7 for more help on researching a school option.

P A R T

2

Making the
Best Choice

The Pros and Cons of Today's School Choices

by Jim Mhoon

*Do not train children to learn by force or harshness, but direct them
to it by what amuses their minds, so that you may be better able
to discover with accuracy the peculiar bent of the genius of each.*
—PLATO

*This is what the Lord says: "Stand at the crossroads and look;
ask for the ancient paths, ask where the good way is,
and walk in it, and you will find rest for your souls."*
—JEREMIAH 6:16

A rmed with principles for school choice success, it's time to begin surveying the various options commonly available around the country. While we would like to see an increase in school choice nationwide, most parents throughout the United States can find some form of choice in their communities.

In an ideal world, we'd have clear-cut choices. Our children would maximize their learning under the best academics, would attend school without fear of physical harm, and would have their values affirmed.

Schools are just like the rest of the world, however; they're full of shades of gray. This chapter will help you grasp some of the pros and cons of the various environments with the goal of assisting you in the selection process. First, let's talk about a few principles to keep in mind when evaluating the strengths and weaknesses of each environment.

1. *Education is about much more than simply attaining knowledge.* It is as much about *how* to learn as it is *what* to learn. Therefore, your choice of academic environment must teach students learning skills as well as deliver knowledge.

2. *Education is also about attainment of skills that will lead to success in all areas of life.* Therefore, academic programs must either directly provide a varied experience or accommodate alternative experiences in some other setting. For example, speaking in front of a group of people is a valuable skill. A student can learn how to research, outline, and deliver a speech without ever interacting with other students. Delivering the speech, however, is no theoretical matter. The student needs to do so in front of a group in order to master the skill.

3. Not all families have the same list of priorities pertaining to education. An environment that works well for one family may not work at all for another. The key is to understand your family priorities and your child's needs and then identify the school that will best fit each.

Public Schools

Public schools are best defined as government-funded schools, run by local school boards beholden to state board of education oversight. They are part of the government system that provides equal opportunity for education to all residents within district boundaries. As such, public schools are secular institutions and currently are limited in their ability to address the religious needs of their students.

Dr. Paul Hill from the University of Washington believes, "Public education is not defined by school boards that act as little legislatures,

---

Signs of a Good Program

Great education programs share several distinct characteristics:

- They have a clear mission and guiding principles.
- They have high expectations of students.
- They monitor progress.
- They adjust to the child's learning styles and needs.
- They focus on effective learning tasks.
- They have a strong connection between home and school.
- They are safe and orderly.
- They are well-led and well-staffed by qualified people.

by categorical funding, by civil service employment of teachers, or by government monopoly. Public education rests on something deeper, a permanent American commitment to educating children by whatever means work."[1]

Much of the criticism leveled at public schools today is well earned. Parents have many concerns about public school including physical safety, academic rigor, secularization, and even indoctrination to controversial subjects that often offend religious and moral beliefs. It should be noted, however, that public schools are responsible for, and credited with, educating millions of Americans . . . people who read, write, do math, vote, and raise great kids. Furthermore, public schools are staffed by our neighbors, friends, siblings, spouses, church volunteers, and fellow citizens. These teachers are also among the most educated in our society and many of them report a true sense of calling to their field.

Under the category of public schools there are several variations:

Neighborhood Schools

Public schools used to be strictly defined by neighborhood schools that were assigned according to boundaries drawn up by the school board. Children were assigned a school according to their physical address. Most adults today grew up in this school environment. Personally, I have good memories of my public school experience and few complaints about the quality of the programs I encountered. I appreciated the diversity of the student body and enjoyed being part of the broader community. Unfortunately, I know people who grew up in more urban environments who cringe at the thought of attending their neighborhood school. In some cases, neighborhood schools work exactly as intended; in others they fall way short of expectations. Neighborhood schools are still very common manifestations in public school districts, but not quite the monopolies of past generations. Interestingly, neighborhood schools have actually been passive recipients of parental choice for many years. Fully 63 percent of Americans exercise some form of choice.[2] Some parents apply for an out-of-district permit in order to place their child in a particular school. Others choose to live within the defined boundaries of a neighborhood school with a good reputation. This is precisely why your zoned school has an effect on the value of your home. Schools with good reputations actually drive home prices up as parents compete for residences that guarantee placement in desirable schools.

Personally, we have found neighborhood schools to be a blessing for our circumstance. We have a son, Kyle, with special needs who requires significant accommodation. Private schools are unable to accommodate him. Our neighborhood schools found ways to work with Kyle and established an individual education plan (also known as an IEP) meant to set goals and create the best environment possible for his needs. IEPs may generate controversy, but they are honest attempts to make the very most of resources available for children that need special attention.

Pros of Neighborhood Schools

- Neighborhood schools are normally close to home and transportation is provided for students beyond walking distance.

- Neighborhood schools serve families who live in close proximity to one another, and can serve to support a sense of community and provide a ready mix of friends who live nearby.
- As with all public schools, there is no extra cost for enrollment.
- Neighborhood schools are required to serve your family without regard to number of children, economic status, special needs, or language barriers.
- They usually have credentialed teachers or teachers in the process of getting a credential.
- They use objective measures of education effectiveness via standardized tests and comparative data.
- Public schools normally have more extracurricular options than most private schools.

Cons of Neighborhood Schools

- Parent involvement can vary widely. As the neighborhood school is the default for local families, many simply enroll in the school that is most convenient and fail to invest further.
- Unless it is a magnet program, neighborhood schools don't have the benefit of attracting students and families with specific common interests, abilities, or needs.
- As a public school, there are risks associated with political or ideological agendas and viewpoints that might offend your beliefs or family values.
- Sometimes too much emphasis is placed on standardized tests.
- Class size can become a problem in this environment.

Magnet Schools

There have always been differences in the quality of schools both within districts and across districts. One of the more glaring examples in U.S. history had its roots in segregation and resulted in persistent ethnic and socioeconomic achievement gaps. The problem became so great (in some ways it still is) that in the 1960s the U.S. government required that students from segregated schools be bused into higher-performing schools. The theory was that desegregated schools would normalize academically, and the schools previously populated mostly by lower socioeconomic students would achieve similar academic standing as those populated by middle-class students. "Busing" was terribly unpopular in America, and it led in part to the development of magnet schools.

Originally, magnets were conceived as academically attractive programs that would entice enrollment across ethnic lines, with the

Magnetic Attraction

Have you ever noticed how much faster time goes by when you are engaged in an activity you find interesting or fun? Did you have that experience when you were a student? Many people report on personal experiences where they struggled in a class they perceived as "boring," sometimes barely squeaking by on grades, only to ace another class they found interesting. If a magnet program is a fit, there is greater potential that children will encounter more classes they find interesting, and the possibility of their thriving academically skyrockets.

hope that parents would opt to send their children to a school populated by various racial groups. Many magnet programs still have ethnic diversity as their primary selection criteria. Magnets have also
been established around other interests that have little to do with ethnic diversity and now appeal to interests such as arts or technology.
The net effect is programs that appeal to special interests within the
student population and education philosophies that are often different from more traditional schools. Some districts have magnet programs that provide customized services for children with special
needs—for example, the deaf and hard of hearing, those who speak
English as a second language, and the gifted and talented.

Other districts have become so "magnetized" that virtually every
school in the district has a distinct flavor, and they operate under an
open-enrollment structure in which every family has the right and is
encouraged to select a school based upon their preference. There are
still neighborhood boundaries, but they exist as a default rather than
as a primary filter. I once lived in a city where every school in the district had a unique angle on education, offering programs as varied as
advanced placement, technology, International Baccalaureate, music,
drama, architecture, and hands-on science. Families were encouraged
to select programs across the district based upon their own preferences.

Pros of Magnet Schools

- Generally speaking, the more intentional parents are about
  selecting a school, the more involved they are in the education
  process. Greater parental involvement strengthens schools.
  Magnets are opt-in programs for families outside of the normal

zone, so they tend to have a higher proportion of intentional families than a standard public school.

- Magnet programs have the potential of providing added motivation for students who have an interest in the area the magnet specializes in.

- Ideally, magnet programs attract staff and administration who have an ideological bent for customized programs. Hence, the chance for personality matches and common interest bonds are heightened.

- Social/ethnic diversity may be increased in this environment.

Cons of Magnet Schools

- Sometimes the specialty of a particular magnet program is not conducive to family goals, children's learning styles, or ideological differences.

- Every once in a while a magnet program is established that is a bad idea, is not managed well, or simply doesn't meet the desired goals of the program.

- Magnet programs are not always well-defended when budget issues arrive, new administrations take over, or state laws change.

Charter Schools

Charter schools (also known as community schools) are government-financed schools operated by nongovernmental entities. Typically, they share two distinguishing traits: (1) The entity operating the school is independent of any school district and is not a governmental agency, and (2) they do not serve students within specific attendance boundaries. State charters serve students throughout the state, and district charters serve students throughout the district and allow interdistrict transfers as they are available.

Charter schools are similar to magnet schools in that they seek to appeal to families on the basis of: (1) a unique educational approach, such as classical education or expedition learning; (2) the special needs of families or the community, such as Edison schools, which target low achieving segments of a community or virtual home-based schools such as K-12; and (3) a particular discipline, such as art, humanities, science, or technology. Charter schools can be small, independent operations or part of a large education company. Some of them are for-profit institutions and some are run by the government.

Like other public schools, charters cannot discriminate based upon race or religion and they must comply with laws restricting religious instruction. However, they seek to distinguish themselves from the regular district model by providing a specialized approach to education. They are also managed separately from the local district with their own board of directors.

Charter schools are similar to magnet programs in that they are opt-in programs populated by students who have chosen to attend the school. Generally, this is a positive indicator of parental involvement. It is vital for parents to understand the charter of a given school and its approach to education. For example, some charter schools seek to serve students who have not managed well in traditional environments. For a high-achieving student, such an environment may not be suitable. Others seek to provide an advanced curriculum or focus on experiential learning or appeal to certain learning styles.

The effectiveness of charter schools is a subject of debate, with some claiming that charters have not demonstrated adequate improvement over more traditional models. Proponents suggest that many charters purposefully appeal to the neediest students. Meanwhile, some programs are setting new standards in education and out-performing all but the very best, advanced curriculum models. As with other public programs, the true test is whether the particular program in consideration meets the standards you have. You should expect good academics, good parent involvement and direction, qualified teachers, and adequate facilities.

Pros of Charter Schools

- Some of the more innovative education systems have arisen from the ranks of charter schools. In some cases, charter programs have academically outdistanced their public school peers considerably.
- Charter programs are 100 percent opt-in, which could mean greater parental involvement.
- Charter programs are funded based upon student enrollment and must find a particular niche in the community in order to compete with established programs. Consequently, they tend to have greater accountability to parents.

- Charter schools are usually run by independent boards elected by the families of that school, and they often require that board members have students of their own in the school. This maximizes accountability.

Cons of Charter Schools

- There are lots of ideas out there on building a better school. Some of them are good, some of them are not. New programs come with a set of risks that are often difficult to discern.
- Charter schools normally do not receive 100 percent of the funding per student that traditional public schools receive. Financial viability is often a major issue with charter operations.
- Charter schools are often political footballs; they are not approved in all states, and some states impose arbitrary rules on charters, making operation and long-term viability questionable. For example, California changed charter laws a few years ago in the middle of the school year and removed funds from some schools, leaving families scrambling to enroll in a new program.
- Charters are not always constrained by state laws requiring teaching credentials. This can result in teachers who are not well qualified for the job. On the other hand, many are exceptional teachers who have not run the gauntlet of state credentialing. The problem is that there are no objective criteria for assessing a teacher's suitability for the classroom.

• Not all charters use standardized testing to measure academic progress. This makes it difficult to measure their effectiveness against other alternatives. On the other hand, many charters cater to the neediest students and so start at a disadvantage with respect to standardized tests. It's important to know the difference between a school hesitant to be measured and a school that is being measured from a disadvantaged position.

Private Schools

Private schools are both elective and selective. They are elective in that all students must choose to attend, but they are selective in that only those who can afford to pay are able to attend. Often the elective process narrows student candidates to those who have a particular affinity for an institution, religious denomination, community, or future goal. As such, many private school students have at least some shared interest. The student body is also made up of children whose families have the awareness and wherewithal to provide for a private school experience. Thus, they can be perceived as being economically advantaged. That is not necessarily the case, however; many private schools are dependent upon student recruitment and have a variety of programs to assist families. Private-school administrators often encourage families to inquire even if they don't believe the school is affordable. There is often financial aid or other assistance available for motivated families.

Some private schools are highly creative in their development of curriculum while others utilize curriculum developed for the general market, or "third-party" curriculum. Teacher credentials vary widely as they are not bound by state standards. Essentially, private schools are more beholden to the marketplace, not external standards. In this sense, it is important to investigate the voluntary accountability oversight schools submit themselves to. Look for accrediting bodies and regional organizations such as the North Central Association of Colleges and Schools, or private accrediting bodies such as the Association of Christian Schools International. These associations require member schools to meet minimum standards in terms of academic achievement, testing, teacher credentials, curriculum, and facilities.

One of the main advantages of private schools is their freedom to include religious instruction as part of their elective and required curriculum. Many private schools have behavioral standards to which students must ascribe. Others require a statement of faith or other sign of allegiance to a particular set of beliefs. Many private Christian schools place a special emphasis on community service, mission trips, and calling from God, and even have as a goal to raise up future Christian leaders. Even so, it is important to remember that enrolling children in a private school is no substitute for parent involvement and diligence.

The term "private school" may conjure images of expensive, high-class, college preparatory boarding schools, and such institutions do exist. Most private schools in the United States, however, are small, modest operations with limited facilities. While there are secular private schools, the overwhelming majority are affiliated with religious institutions. Some private schools are part of a large, well-organized structure such as Catholic or Lutheran schools; others are small, independent operations tied only to a local church. Typically, schools associated with denominational structures (for example, Catholic schools) are more predictable than independent schools, whose curriculum, accreditation, and academic oversight vary widely.

Private schools are governed by their own set of rules. These rules may be established by a local board or may be imposed from the national organization or denomination. It is sometimes difficult to tell which set of operational rules—national or local—hold the advantage. On one hand, local control means nimble response to the community need; on the other hand, association with strong national organizations ensures that the school is meeting standards set for it by the national body.

Things to Look for in Private Schools

1. *Associations and accreditations.* Unless the administration is exceptionally skilled, it is usually important for a private school to have applied for and been accepted into a governing set of standards and achieved some sort of accreditation. That is the seal of approval that says the school meets certain standards of financial accountability, academic rigor, rules of ethics, and so on. For examples, see page 206.

2. *Curriculum.* Some schools employ teachers who are trained and skilled educators. They are able to create and deploy effective curriculum

and tie that curriculum to state or governing association standards. Other schools simply adopt a curriculum created by third-party curriculum providers and implement them in their system.

3. *Academic accountability.* Public schools are required to use standardized tests to demonstrate student competence in core subjects. Many private schools choose to use the same tests in order to compare their program to public schools, while others select an independent testing norm that measures student achievement but is difficult to compare to state standards. Still others choose to not use standardized tests at all. When evaluating a school that does not use standardized tests, get data on SAT or ACT scores and compare them with surrounding public schools. College placement statistics are also good indicators of academic suitability.

4. *Denomination or religious affiliation.* You'll want to ensure that the religious viewpoint of the school is consistent with your personal beliefs.

Pros of Private Schools

- Participation is by choice. Parents should have a high degree of commitment to the school and this factor significantly contributes to creating a good academic and social environment.
- Private schools can legally provide religious instruction.
- Private schools aren't dependent on the state for money, and therefore may have better control over their long-term budgeting process than charter or magnet schools.
- Private schools have to compete with free public schools. Ideally, their accountability to parents should be high.

- Private schools may tend to attract like-minded families, making social interaction with others easier.

Cons of Private Schools

- Private schools require parents to pay tuition for their children to attend.
- Teachers may not be required to have state certification.
- Because private schools charge tuition and therefore may not be an option for lower-income families, the student population may not be as diverse as in a public-school setting.
- There is no accountability to state standards unless it is self-imposed.
- Often there is no bus service.
- Sports, music, and other special-interest activities may not be offered.
- Sometimes there is a long waiting period to get your child enrolled.

Homeschool

Homeschooling has a long tradition in the United States. Abraham Lincoln, Benjamin Franklin, Theodore Roosevelt, and other greats were all educated at home. While a relative outsider on the scene, homeschooling has managed to carve out an important niche and establish itself as a credible, viable, and effective means to educate children.

Earning the legal right to homeschool was a hard-fought battle in some states, and continues to be challenged. Most states, however, now recognize the right of parents to educate their children at home. There are legal variations relating to state accountability requirements and meeting state education standards. Parents of homeschooled high school students also need to consider college recognition and acceptance standards.

Homeschool is difficult to define because it takes on so many different forms. Some homeschool families literally create their own curriculum and find nontraditional means to educate their children that range from creative to out-and-out strange. Other homeschool families purchase and use services or packaged curriculums that are highly regimented and structured. Still others use blends of various techniques including the ones already mentioned.

Above all other education methods, homeschooling requires the most from parents. Their involvement is key to success and is often intense and challenging. Commitment level, available time, and teaching skills are significant factors to be considered before parents begin homeschooling. Today's marketplace provides unprecedented support for homeschoolers, making this option more feasible than ever.

One of the major objections to homeschooling is a supposed lack of socialization of children. This objection is based on the observation that children who spend most of their time at home do not have daily interaction with their peers like their institutional counterparts. Supporters of homeschool point out that there are many relational alternatives to six-hour days at school and they have taken action to intentionally provide their students with activities that include most, if not all, of the options available to students in more traditional schools. Today, homeschooled children participate in athletic teams, academic competition, band, and the like. They also enjoy freedom to learn through experience and real-life interaction such as travel, field trips, and internships. Progressive homeschool practices have all but debunked the socialization objection.

Generally, in academics homeschooled students compare favorably to their public- and private-schooled peers. But the variance between students can be great. The key is a skilled parent-teacher who is up to the task and who utilizes available resources to maximize the opportunities. In the past, homeschool families were on their own and had to create or discover curriculum and material for instruction. Many families still opt for a homegrown approach, but there are many excellent homeschool organizations that provide curriculum, teacher training, parent and student support, and even cooperative learning programs. Some you can research include Alpha Omega Publishers, Sonlight Curriculum, K-12, A Beka, and Bob Jones Home School for curriculum, and for local homeschool associations for direct connection and support.

Homeschool families have complete latitude to provide religious instruction without limitations. Successful families have a good plan, good support, and a passion for their work. The keys are intentionality and sufficient knowledge to lead a long-term education process.

Trends in homeschool include the following options:

1. *Homeschool/public-school blends.* Many public schools allow students to enroll in selected classes. Typically, these are math and science classes that require higher skilled teachers or special facilities.

2. *Homeschool/private-school blends.* Many private schools offer similar services as public schools. These services may include offering homeschool families with a la carte classes that require more teacher expertise, a group environment, or perhaps lab facilities.

Other private schools utilize a homeschool blend in order to expand student population without adding facilities. An emerging program called University Model Schools, for example, is an intentional homeschool/private school blend that specifically assigns education curriculum to both the home and classroom. This approach is intended to create a collegelike setting that uses both self-study and classroom instruction.

3. *Homeschool associations.* These are best described as cooperatives in which parents collaborate to provide education collectively to their children. The variations in associations include parents teaching a particular discipline to a group of students and pooling their time and talents to organize field trips, sports leagues, music programs, and other group events. Essentially, they strive to provide the services normally found in an institutional school.

Often these homeschool associations use church facilities. For example, on most Thursday mornings if you walk into New Life Church in Colorado Springs, Colorado, you'll find yourself in the middle of a throng of elementary-age children. They will be working on art projects, writing stories, participating in plays, moving from classroom to classroom, and engaging in multiple learning activities.

You are not walking into a private school; you have arrived on the day when the local homeschool association meets. It is a chance for collaboration and fun and learning on a major scale. Think of it as an educational swap meet.

4. *Virtual schools.* Many children are being taught at home via computer and with curriculum that is controlled out of a central facility. They have instructors, assignments, and other activities much like a classroom setting, but their classroom is in their home. Parent involvement in such programs is significant, but not as much as other homeschool methods. Virtual schools can be private schools or even charter schools providing services into the home. The common denominators that define virtual schools are the central importance of the computer as the learning and interaction tool, and the centralized control of assignments by the virtual school operator.

5. *Homeschool curriculum providers.* There was a time when homeschoolers were left on their own to create a curriculum. Some still opt to do it themselves, but it's no longer necessary. There is a variety of for-profit and not-for-profit companies that develop curriculum for use by homeschooling families. The approaches are wide-ranging. Typically, these programs provide all of the material and instructions a family needs to create a robust home education program.

Pros of Homeschooling
- Flexibility with curriculum. It can be tailored exactly to what your child needs.
- Increased "face time" with your children.
- Daily opportunities to incorporate spiritual/biblical material.

- Flexibility with sports, arts, music, etc.
- Have better control over peer influence.

Cons of Homeschooling
- Usually there is a greater demand on the parent's time.
- Increased expense if you're not using state-provided curriculum.
- Special activities may require more effort to pursue.
- Students may not be exposed to "expert" teachers.
- Homeschooling may require that a portion of your house be devoted to a school room.

A Word about Public Schools versus Private Schools or Homeschools

When considering the academic environment for your child, consider your ultimate goal for his or her life and place the decisions you are making in perspective. From a spiritual perspective, ask yourself questions such as these: Is it enough that your child is saved or knows the meaning of Jesus' death on the cross and His lordship? Do you desire to raise a child who is able to contribute to the Great Commission and share his or her spiritual gifts with the entire community? If you select a program that isolates your child from those who do not know God, how will you provide relational opportunities for the "lost" to meet your child?

It is easy to insulate our families from any real relationships outside of the body of Christ, and that sets a dangerous precedent. Whatever you do, don't throw your child to the wolves in hostile public or private schools (if that's what you have in your area), but don't isolate your child in a Christian setting either. Parents need to provide a healthy balance between protecting their children and providing them safe contact with those who don't embrace Christianity.

My Child's Learning Style and Best Learning Environment

by Cheri Fuller

I am always ready to learn,
but I do not always like being taught.
—SIR WINSTON CHURCHILL

Your hands made me and formed me;
give me understanding to learn your commands.
—PSALM 119:73

How do you choose among all the education options available? Making the best choice of those schools depends in great part on discovering your child's learning style and applying it to choosing a learning environment. The second part of this chapter will explain how to discover and build on your child's style for increased learning at home. For now, let's evaluate the schooling options and how to determine which schools are more likely to meet your child's needs.

For example, a workbook-oriented school would not be the best school for an active, hands-on learner. *Doers* tend to burn out and get frustrated if every day is a long marathon of pencil-and-paper activities with more and more worksheets. They need more than a classroom discussion of sculpture and paintings; they need to visit art museums. They need science classes that use labs and teachers who use experiments. They prefer hands-on projects in social studies, manipulatives in math class, and production-oriented assignments for language arts.

One encouraging trend in education has been development schools, where teachers provide strong leadership and learn to use innovative tools to meet the diverse needs of all students and reach "all kinds of minds."[1] The end result is a classroom environment that supports kids in finding success in individualized ways. In one such class, I knew a teacher who was initially frustrated with one student's behavior. After sitting in his chair for a certain amount of time, Jacob would begin to yawn (a red flag that his mental energy was ebbing), then stretch and fidget. Next he would get out of his chair instead of doing his work.

After taking an assessment of his kinesthetic learning style and realizing that she couldn't spend so much time chasing him around and trying to get him to sit down, so she tried a different approach. When Jacob yawned several times, his teacher took that as a cue for a 30-second stretch break for the whole class—which not only helped Jacob but a lot of the other kids as well. She let him take notes to the office and hand out papers from time to time, and so that he wouldn't think less was expected from him than other kids, she assigned him a poster to make or a report to write and present using an area of his strength or interest.

In addition, the reading and computer room had two stationary bikes, and the teacher found that Jacob's reading speed and comprehension improved as he was able to "ride and read." His overall behavior and attention to other tasks improved as well.

Kinesthetic learners are not the only ones who need specialized learning plans. Children with strong auditory/verbal skills—*Talkers*—benefit from classrooms that permit small-group learning, class debates and discussions, oral presentations, chances for writing projects, and concrete experiences to apply what they've learned. Talkers

---

A Slow Starter

Winston Churchill had problems in reading. As a boy he also suffered from a speech defect and was hyperactive, which did not endear him to his teachers. He was placed in the lowest group, where the slow boys were taught English. Yet he became a world leader, a statesman, a great orator, a prolific author who won the Nobel Prize for Literature in 1953, and Prime Minister of England during World War II (1940-45) and 1951-1955.

also thrive on opportunities like producing class newsletters or interviewing family members and recording family stories (a great way to learn history). Auditory/verbal learners need more than just the read-the-textbook, do-a-worksheet, take-a-test process. Also, when teachers provide the material in audio form (such as books on tape) as well as in printed form, or encourage Talkers to use tape recorders in the classroom, it can motivate their learning.

Visual learners—I call them *Watchers*—more than any other students, like to study independently if given the opportunity. They thrive in traditional classrooms, which reward good textbook readers and test takers, but they need opportunities to use their visual skills and creativity as well. Watchers may like to set their own goals, write them down, and pursue independent projects like researching and creating science fair exhibits. Not only do they benefit greatly from having the teacher use PowerPoint presentations with the lessons she orally teaches, but their learning is enriched by having a chance to create their own PowerPoint and overhead slides.

Providing time in computer labs to learn word processing and other skills holds benefits for all students, because it can involve all three senses: seeing, saying, and doing—but visual and kinesthetic kids especially thrive on it.

Tapping into Kids' Learning Styles for Reading Programs

Learning style needs to be considered when evaluating the kind of reading instruction program the school provides for children in the lower grades. If your child is strongly auditory, a phonics learn-to-read program will likely be beneficial. Phonics instruction is needed for all kids so that they can master word decoding, but this is especially true for Talkers. Some visual kids could master reading with the old look-say, sight-word method because it's based on visual cues and sight-word recognition. These same kids, however, could probably teach themselves to read with billboard signs on the highway.

But if your child has kinesthetic strengths, he may likely need to have hands-on activities added to the phonics reading program, such as tracing his finger in dry Jell-O powder to learn letters or "skywriting" letters to practice the shapes and sounds. When choosing a school, inquire about the type of reading program the school uses to determine if it is the best match for your child. Then at the start of the school year, provide the teacher with information on your child's learning strengths so he or she can plan the best reading instruction approach. If there's a problem, meet with the teacher, and help create an action plan with strategies to shore up your child's weaknesses while bringing components of his or her learning strengths into the existing reading program.

With the huge variety of learn-to-read methods available today (Visual Phonics; computer programs; braille; the Spalding phonics methods; Sing, Spell, Read & Write; and many others), no child should be considered hopeless. While children can benefit from a correct diagnosis, every child can improve his/her skills. Children with all kinds of learning differences and learning disabilities such as dyslexia can become good readers. We need to put our energies into finding the right reading method that builds on each child's learning strengths.

What Are Your Child's Smarts?

The way children learn is also influenced by their intelligence gifts, or what their "smarts" are—whether in the math/science area or language skills, or whether they have musical or spatial gifts, people-smarts, or body-smarts. Because these talents and skills are part of your child's strengths, they are helpful to factor in when you are choosing a school environment.

Success breeds success. Research has shown that doing well in classes that build on talents or gifts improves students' performance in *all* their classes. Why? Because the positive habits that success creates in these courses carry over into other courses and activities. We find that when students have a chance within their school days to utilize and grow in their areas of strength, they tend to thrive and be more motivated learners, even in other areas outside their favorite subjects.

For example, if your child is musically talented, a school with a strong music program would be a good learning environment—not only because she would enjoy developing her musical gifts, but because teachers in a music-oriented school might be more likely to use music in the classroom as a way to strengthen memory and integrate it with social studies or other subjects.

A school like the XYZ School of Arts & Theater would encourage a child's learning if she's talented in dance or drama as well. If your child is body-smart, I would encourage you to *avoid* putting him in a school so small or new that it has no budget, resources, or personnel for sports programs. Unless you can provide sports opportunities outside of the school in community leagues or club teams, your child's learning may be stunted. He needs chances to shine just as much as other kids!

Language-talented kids benefit from a school with debate or journalism opportunities or from foreign language immersion schools, which in some cities begin at the kindergarten level. Many cities have math/science schools for students with analytical and logical abilities, especially at the high school level. With the growth of charter and magnet schools around the nation, more and more schools, even at the elementary level, specialize and focus on specific areas of intelligence.

Avoid Negativity

Most of all, whatever school your child attends, avoid letting an individual teacher, guidance counselor, or school administrator have a negative attitude toward your child because of his learning differences. Sometimes labels, even when they stem from accurate diagnoses, can cause others to have doubts about your child's ability to learn. This attitude hurts kids because it denies them the opportunity to change and develop. Negativity also produces a downward spiral. If teachers and parents lower their expectations of what she can do, this lowers the child's expectations of her potential. With lowered expectations, the student puts out less effort, which leads to lower achievement. Identifying the problem and coming up with an action plan and strategies to help your child compensate and use her strengths are much more effective. Be sure to demonstrate your confidence by showing patience and giving lots of praise.

Because kids' brains are like computers, what they haven't understood this term or semester—if they keep trying and have support and good teaching that takes into account their learning styles—it all comes together and the new information clicks six or nine months or a year later.

Believing in our kids 100 percent in this way and remembering that God has uniquely wired them up and given them gifts and talents make a huge difference. I heard Jim Trelease (author of *The Read-Aloud Handbook*) tell about his brother Brian, who had trouble with reading when he was a boy. In his early years, Brian wasn't the achiever in the family; his three brothers far surpassed him in elementary and high school.

Yet every night their dad, who must have sensed Brian had a spark of business savvy, read the *Wall Street Journal* to him. The author thought, *How silly; Brian doesn't even understand the journal and couldn't read it himself.* It took the longest for Brian to graduate from college. Yet he went on to graduate with honors and get a master's degree, and he was the only one of his brothers to become the CEO of a major corporation. Now Brian's corporation runs ads in the *Wall Street Journal.*[2]

No matter what school your child attends, it's the home environment and parents that have the most impact. As you become more aware of your child's unique talents and learning strengths and help him utilize study strategies that capitalize on these, you'll find he'll become a more active, motivated learner. And with this knowledge and belief in your child's potential, he, too, can achieve amazing things.

How to Discover Your Child's Learning Strengths

"Mom," Amy wailed, "I don't understand this! I'll fail the test!" She slumped in her chair, dejected and frustrated during homework time. A sixth grader, Amy was having trouble memorizing all the parts of a flower and how they relate to pollination. Her teacher had delivered a short lecture, assigned a chapter to read, and given the kids a worksheet to complete. Amy faithfully finished her work, but after all that effort, she feared she still couldn't recall enough information to do well on the test. She was haunted by failure—on the previous week's quiz she had scored only a 60 percent, and now Amy was flattened by discouragement.

Her mother encouraged her to ask for extra help, so Amy stayed after school the next day. Her teacher brought out a red tulip and put it on a white sheet of paper. She cut it in half lengthwise and pointed out the parts of the flower; Amy touched the stamen, filament, pistil, style, ovary, and calyx. Next Amy made a model of a flower and put a different color toothpick on the different parts.

When Mom picked her up, Amy told her what she'd learned. Usually she had trouble explaining things, but with the clay flower she'd made, she communicated clearly and glowed with pride. When Friday's test came, her grade rose to a B.

Amy is a kinesthetic learner, an energetic girl who is talented in math and soccer, and like many bright people including Thomas

Edison, inventor of the lightbulb and phonograph, needs a hands-on approach to processing information and learning.

As I share in my book *Talkers, Watchers, and Doers, Unlocking Your Child's Unique Learning Style,* your child has a learning strength as unique as his or her fingerprint. I've observed this in Amy and scores of kids I've worked with over the years. Learning style means how he or she takes in information and retains it. Some children process infor-

---

How You as a Parent Learn

Imagine you have a job where you will have to learn a new operating system for the computer. You're told to take the rest of the day to learn how to use it and tomorrow you'll be tested. Part of your salary evaluation will be based on how well you master the new operating system. Would you look for someone to explain how to use it and let you ask them questions? (Auditory strength.) Would you carefully read the manual and study the charts and diagrams? (Visual strength.) Or would you put away the manual and instead dive in by trying to figure out how to use it by trial and error? (Kinesthetic strength.)

If your child is stuck and you're trying to teach a concept, would you naturally use words and do a lot of explaining and reading aloud from the textbook? (Auditory strength.) Do you draw a picture or diagram? (Visual strength.) Would you make a demonstration or whip up an experiment to help him understand? (Kinesthetic strength.)

If your teaching style doesn't match your child's learning style, consider adapting your teaching to your child's natural bent. This will save time and frustration in the long run.

mation best by hearing the teacher explain things and then discussing what they learned. Other children's strengths are visual. They can master a spelling list in no time just by seeing the words and picturing them in their mind for the test.

Like Amy's teacher, more and more teachers and schools today are discovering that rather than ignore or fight children's natural learning styles, we can utilize them to help unlock students' learning potential. It's great for educators to have seminars on this topic, but I've found it's even more vital for parents to understand their own and their children's learning styles. Understanding about learning styles not only reduces homework conflict but will help your kids learn and achieve more and assist you in choosing a learning environment where your child can thrive.

In this chapter you'll discover how to identify your child's unique strengths and help him to study in ways that maximize his abilities. Research has shown that the students who make the highest grades know how to utilize these learning-style strengths in the classroom. While some students do this intuitively, all kids can become more active learners and retain information better if they are taught to "study in style."

How to Discover Your Child's Learning Style

Do you need a degree in education to discover your children's strengths? No! You can simply notice how your children tackle problems and express themselves. For example, kids who have visual strengths say things like, "Mom, show me what you mean" or "That doesn't look right; I don't get a clear picture of what you're saying." A hands-on, kinesthetic learner might say, "Walk me through that one step at a time" or "I don't get it; that feels strange." Auditory kids say things like "That doesn't sound right" and "Does this sound better to you?" You can also gain clues by observing eye and body movements. Watchers look into space when they're trying to remember something and stare at illustrations and objects longer than others. If the teacher has been talking and explaining too long, Doers start to drum their fingers on the desk or fidget.

Remember, no two people learn exactly the same way. In fact, you probably have a different way of taking in information than your spouse and at least one of your kids. Check out the sidebar on page 108 to get more of an understanding of your style. Why? Because the more you understand the way *you* learn, the better you can work with your child and eliminate homework conflict. That way, you won't say, "You aren't listening!" when you've explained fractions the fifth time and your daughter still doesn't understand them. You'll know that drawing a picture or using a piece of bread divided into sections will help her get it.

Look at the characteristics of different learners in the section below to determine your child's strengths. Keep in mind that while most kids (about 75 percent) have a primary learning style, some will be combination learners who are strong in two of the three modalities.

Talkers: Kids with Auditory Strengths

Kids who have auditory strengths often talk to themselves or their classmates as they process information, but they are also good listeners. They can listen to their teacher longer than other students their age, love to be read to, like to discuss ideas, and repeat directions. They may have been early chatterboxes who sounded like little adults. They usually have a crisp auditory memory and remember best not just when they see information, but when they hear it, and say or explain it to someone else, such as in a study group.

Our older son had these strengths, and when he began to put them to good use during study time, his grades improved. When he had events and lists of dates for a history test to memorize, I suggested he read the questions onto a blank tape (pausing between each one), then use the recording to practice the information. By tapping into his learning strengths—his auditory and verbal channels—he made one of the highest grades on the test, but most importantly, discovered a new way to study. He later used this technique to memorize long poems.

Here are some ways you can help your child with auditory strengths:

Make a study tape. This study strategy can be used in many subjects, from learning multiplication tables to Spanish vocabulary or states and capitals—but it yields great results. Get flash cards from a learning store or have your child make her own, with a question on one side and answer on the other. To make the tape, the child asks a question into the microphone, waits a few seconds, and then goes on to the next question until they're all recorded. After the tape is made, the child plays it back and tries to say the answer following each question.

Convert information to be learned into a poem, acrostic, rap, or rhyme. For example, "Thirty days has September, April, June, and November" or H-O-M-E-S for the Great Lakes: Huron, Ontario, Michigan, Erie, and Superior.

Study with a partner or group. They can discuss the material, teach each other key concepts, debate issues, and then pick questions for a practice test they can take and score.

Modify the material. If a homework lesson is visual (such as reading a complicated chapter from the science book), you can make it auditory by reading it aloud together or letting your child recite it onto a blank tape, which she can later use for review.

Doers: Kids with Kinesthetic Strengths

Doers tend to try everything out by doing and touching; that's also how they learn best—by a hands-on approach. One young woman I know is now a registered nurse, but in her growing-up years, she had more energy than most children, not to mention more than the tired adults who tried to keep up with her! Doers, or *Movers* as I often think of them, often shine on the athletic field—it's as though they have computers in their brains timing their movements and coordination; or they have the skillful small-muscle, eye-hand coordination needed for creating intricate projects. But these kids may begin to tune out or misbehave if they have to sit for long periods and get bored if all they do during class are worksheet and pencil-and-paper assignments.

Doers have a harder time remembering oral directions, and they need a lot of physical affection to perform their best (or they go to school and pinch and push other classmates trying to get the physical contact they lack from home). They are active, bright kids who can become achievers and motivated learners if parents or teachers show them how to harness their strengths.

If you're blessed with a Doer, try some of the following learning strategies and watch your child shine:

Whiteboard magic. Get a big whiteboard for your child's room. On it, he can write spelling words or math problems with big letters, or ask him to teach you or his siblings the information. I've seen kids' grades go up just by actively teaching someone the material after reviewing it in the book or notes for 10 to 15 minutes. Doers can become some of the best teachers.

Provide direct, concrete experiences. Lab experiments, field trips, and role-playing help Doers understand information. They'll learn a lot more about electricity if they do an experiment first and *then* read about it and do a worksheet. To learn the parts of a cell, make one out of clay and things found in the kitchen. Let your children put it together and take it apart until they know all the essentials.

Promote active learning. While practicing multiplication tables, your child can bounce a basketball in the driveway (or shoot baskets with a Nerf ball inside on a rainy day). Help your hands-on learner create a board game with the information. He can make a spinner, use cardboard for the playing surface, add some playing pieces and cards in the middle with questions and answers, and then study while having fun. Card games (crazy eights, spades, etc.) also teach kids lots of math concepts and thinking skills like sequencing, computing, logic, and problem solving.

Modify the material. If your child has a sheet of math problems and doesn't understand the concepts behind them, provide concrete objects to touch as she figures and computes. For example, to explain fractions, cut a pizza into sections, or give her beans, buttons, or any kind of manipulative to count. Have her make a study tape (an auditory strategy) but put it on an iPod or portable tape player so she can practice the information while jumping rope.

Watchers: Kids with Visual Strengths

Watchers have such good visual memories it's as though they have copy machines in their minds that help them remember spelling words and other facts after looking at them for a short time. They learn best by *seeing* information on charts, lists, diagrams, and in books. They tend to notice details other kids their own age (and sometimes adults) miss; they also may love puzzles, doing artwork, or building models from directions and diagrams. They may be quieter in class and not volunteer answers, but it doesn't mean they aren't smart. They just tend to mentally analyze the concepts and don't need a lot of verbal or group interaction to comprehend and retain the key ideas.

Here are some ways to capitalize on your child's visual strengths:

Picture it. When events and their dates need to be memorized for a history test, encourage your child to make an illustrated time line, where the dates are written above a simple stick-figure illustration of the event. Pictures and graphics can help your child understand and recall important facts. He could make a diagram or "mental map" with the key concept in the middle circle (the Civil War, for instance) and draw spokes leading to circles with questions and room for answers in each one. Focus on the key "W" questions: Who? What? Why? Where? and When? A mental map is a great way for a child to picture, understand, and remember the information.

Emphasize with color. Encourage your child to highlight in colors to categorize facts. For example, to learn parts of speech, he can use a green highlighter to indicate nouns, yellow for verbs, blue for adjectives, and pink for adverbs. Have him use colored highlighters to color-code information in the textbook chapter as he reads. Study cards can be made out of bright-colored index cards to help learn material in just about any subject—math, a foreign language, or geography. He can put the cards for this week's test in a plastic bag, carry them through the day, and read over them when there's a break in class work or a line to wait in, and by Friday, the information is learned.

Use computer games to build skills. More than any other, this generation of children is very computer savvy, and kids with visual skills are some of the greatest fans of computer games. Many educators successfully use games like The Lemonade Stand to give kids opportunities to learn real business skills as they order their materials, practice using money, and run a small company. Many parents and teachers like Zoombini's Logical Journey, which is a computer program that builds and strengthens reasoning and analytical skills. Kids can also hone graph-reading skills, learn prealgebra basics, and learn how to analyze data—all while they're having fun on the computer. Parent supervision, of course, is needed for all computer use, and the "screen time" (including TV and movies) needs to be limited and kept in balance with active play, time with family, helping with chores, doing homework, church activities, etc. Visual (and kinesthetic) kids, while benefiting from computer learning, can also become too dependent on the visual stimulation of the computer or the action of video games.

Modify the material. Watchers can also enjoy using their artistic talents to make a board game with a study buddy, create their own organizational methods for class assignments if the one the teacher suggests doesn't work, or benefit from using a whiteboard to outline a chapter and to teach the material to someone else (described in the "Doer" section). Anytime we combine two or three modalities (visual, kinesthetic, and auditory, in the case of the whiteboard teaching strategy), we make the learning and retention even stronger.

■ ■ ■

After reading over the descriptions of clues to learning styles and study methods, talk about them with your child, and demonstrate or try one or two. Then encourage him to make up his own list of "Things I Can Do When I Study" when there's new or difficult information to learn. It may take an investment of your time to teach your children these skills, but you and they will reap the benefits as your kids grow into more confident, active, and independent learners.

Researching Your Family's School Options

by Susan Martins Miller

The mediocre teacher tells.
The good teacher explains.
The superior teacher demonstrates.
The great teacher inspires.
—William Arthur Ward

I will teach you about the power of God;
the ways of the Almighty I will not conceal.
—Job 27:11

W e can't help your son."

These were not the words Barb wanted to hear. Her daughter was doing well at a local charter school—but her son didn't fit in. The teachers tried all the educational tricks up their sleeves, but in the end they concluded that they were not helping him. His test scores were low and his unusual behavior was taking its toll on classroom management. Barbara's son has Asperger's syndrome, one of a spectrum of disorders related to autism. Although his symptoms are fairly mild, he needed more than the charter school could give. Barbara began the process of assessing other options.

A mother of any child can have similar issues. Michael spent second grade in a new school, and the teacher gave his mother, Michelle, no indication he was struggling in reading. His grades and attitude were fine. When Michael's third-grade teacher assessed him, however, he told Michelle that Michael was a full year behind in his reading. Michelle was concerned that the second-grade teacher had not adequately supported Michael in this crucial area of learning, and she was reluctant to keep her two younger children in the same school. Would failure repeat itself? What else could she do?

Michelle was in an optimal position for change. Three public elementary schools were within a 10-minute drive of her home. The district also fully supported homeschool options, complete with free textbooks and partial enrollment options for sports and the arts. Additionally, a small Christian school nearby emphasized "the basics." The options for Michelle's family were plentiful.

Barbara, on the other hand, had fewer choices. She needed special-ed gurus—people experienced with Asperger's syndrome or staff members who were at least willing to become educated and help her come up with realistic solutions.

Imagine school choices on shelves in the store with tags touting the distinct features of each model. If you've ever chosen a new printer to use with your computer, you know the feeling of going from one to another, reading the brochures, and trying to sort out what this one has that the others don't. Some features are more important to you than others. Some features are more affordable. How do you get the most value for what you can afford?

Choosing a school is a lot like that. Understanding what the tags say can be mind-boggling: teaching philosophy, curriculum, extracurricular activities, accreditation, after-school programs, statistics, student-teacher ratio—how do you sort it all out and make the best choice for your family?

Priorities—A Personal Matter

"Boys will be boys." "All kids go through that stage." "She'll outgrow it." "You just have to be firm; kids will learn to obey."

We tend to categorize kids in ways that say we expect them to be more alike than different. Learn to read by age 6. Know the multiplication table by 8. Write an organized three-paragraph essay by 11. The truth is, not all 6-year-olds, 8-year-olds, or 11-year-olds are the same. Whether an educational option is appropriate depends on the needs of your child and family. You get to set the standard. Dream of the ideal setting for your child's learning. Of course, reality is that you'll have to compromise, just as you do with a computer printer.

Setting your priorities will help you know what you're willing to give on and what you must have.

Here are some basic guidelines for determining what's right for your child.

You know your child. Given time, a good teacher will figure out most of the kids in the class and know what works with each of them. Parents have a head start. You know a lot of things about your child that the school won't know going in—or may never discover. These include the following:

- *Learning styles.* Some kids learn better on the go. Others love to sit still with a book. See chapter 6 for more information on learning styles.
- *Temperament.* Kids can be mellow or easily agitated, sensitive or oblivious to others' comments, easily frustrated or tolerant of challenges.
- *Social skills and emotional maturity.* How well does your child play with other kids? Does she handle her anger constructively? Does he interact appropriately for his age?
- *Spiritual maturity.* Perhaps your child thinks about deeper questions or has a closer sense of God than other kids of the same age.
- *Family issues.* On Janet's first day of kindergarten, her father died unexpectedly. A child may hear parents argue every night, and no one else knows it. Perhaps Mom was in the hospital for most of the summer. A rebellious older sibling may be sapping the parents' energy. Children don't leave things like this

at home when they head out the door for school. Teachers won't know what's happening at your house, but you do.

- *Special interests.* Has your daughter got soccer on the mind— constantly? Did your son pick up an older sibling's musical instrument and figure it out on his own? Being in a school that affirms special interests can make all the difference in a child's educational experience.

You know your family's needs. When it was time for Adam to go to kindergarten, Sharon enrolled her son in the public school down the street from her day-care provider so he would have transportation. As a teacher, Andrea enrolled her kids at the school where she taught, rather than their neighborhood school. When she left teaching, she worked out a bus route that would drop her children near her new office.

Scott and Angie enrolled their daughter in a private Christian kindergarten. They knew they could not sustain the expense more than one year, however, and when first grade came, they again faced a choice among affordable options. They chose homeschooling.

Derek and C. C.'s daughter was not faring well in public school, so they enrolled her in a private school. Their son thrived in public school. Different kids have different needs, even in the same family.

Whether it's ease of transportation, convenient location, financial commitments, or multiple children with multiple needs, only you can decide what realities will work in your family.

You know your educational expectations. School is not strictly about what happens in the classroom academically. Your opinions about nonacademic issues may tilt the scale in one direction or another.

Halfway through middle school, Dianna told her mother she was tired of all the swearing in the halls and the ways that people talked about God. She wanted to go to school in a place where she wasn't intimidated about expressing her Christian beliefs. A Christian school was the right place for Dianna at that age. Some families choose Christian schools not because they lack confidence in the public schools, but to ensure that kids develop a solid foundation for faith. Another mother, Nancy, attended Christian schools and now wants to continue the tradition with her son. She faces the financial challenge of finding the funds to realize her dream of sending her son to a Christian school.

Clearly some schools are more traditional in their approach to teaching children, and that may be important to you. On the other hand, you might be fascinated by the idea of an innovative method or focus. Johanna, a homeschooling mom, was in a master's program. As part of a curriculum project, she visited a new charter school centered on the arts. Her son tagged along and decided he liked the idea of this school and wanted to attend. Later he transferred to another school that emphasized math and science through studying aviation.

Some schools, especially private or charter schools, expect a serious level of parental involvement. Others expect less. You have to decide what you can give. You may feel more comfortable in a school where teachers have years of experience rather than putting your child in a teacher's first class out of college. Ask yourself if the overall sociocultural experience matters. When Liz was little, she went to school in northern Illinois in an ethnically mixed neighborhood. When her family moved to a more homogeneous city in central Colorado, her mother was disappointed to lose the ethnic exposure her daughter once had.

Denise's family lived in the San Francisco area. About the time Denise hit fifth grade, the curriculum included stories like "Johnny has two mommies and they live in the same house." Her mother emphatically did not want Denise exposed to ideas that clearly conflicted with her biblical beliefs. Finding private schools to be beyond their financial resources, they ventured into homeschooling. Denise loved it and was educated all the way through high school at home.

Different Kids, Different Choices

Choosing a school is not a cut-and-dried decision. The final decision is a mix of objective data and intuition. Look at each option from multiple angles. And whether you're considering public or private schools, be aware of the information available before making a decision.

Statistics. School districts everywhere measure success by performance on standardized tests, school report cards (how the state assesses the school), and state ratings compared to other similar schools. Many school district administrative offices will have information organized into pie charts and statistical columns. The information appears in an objective way, and you can compare academic performance. If you have that kind of brain, you're in good shape! You can find out what percentage of students in a school met or exceeded the state's goals by grade and by subject—and worlds of other ency-clopedic information.

Dig a little deeper with the school district or the state office of education and you'll also uncover information such as average years of experience for teachers in a specific school, average salary, pupil-to-teacher ratios, teacher ethnic mix, and percentage of teachers with advanced training (beyond college). This information also comes in tabulated formats, but its meaning may be open to interpretation. Do school districts that offer higher salaries necessarily draw better-qualified teachers? Does holding a master's degree necessarily mean the teacher is better than one who has only a bachelor's? What might the rate of teacher turnover in a particular school mean?

Translation, Please

You have an armful of statistics, but you have no idea what they mean! When comparing schools, most of us instinctively jump to looking for the highest academic performance on standardized tests. The more telling number to look for is the growth or gains of students over time. Growth scores reflect how much students learned rather than where they stand in comparison to other students.

Compare a school's performance with other schools that have similar student bodies. Statistics will show ethnic background, income level, mobility rate, class size, teacher profiles, operating expense per student, and other factors that affect the overall quality of a school. Make sure you're comparing apples to apples before drawing conclusions.

Special features. Numbers don't tell the whole story. Schools sometimes offer special programs, and you may not find out about them unless you specifically look and ask. The middle school a mile down the road in the unassuming 30-year-old building may be a magnet school attracting students interested in the arts. The one in the neighborhood across town draws students interested in math and science. When they pour out the doors after the three o'clock bell, the elementary kids all look the same. While chatting with other parents, you discover that the school hosts a program for gifted and talented students in the fourth and fifth grades from all over the district. Ask at the school district office about special offerings across the district, not just in your neighborhood.

As your child gets older, search out the programs that match changing needs. For instance, some middle and high schools offer Achievement Via Individual Determination (AVID). This program, which many educators have used successfully, helps average students boost their performance and prepare for college. Some areas use it across the district, others in select schools, others not at all. In the same public school district, one high school may have twice as many honors and advanced placement classes as another. Your child might be well suited to an aggressive International Baccalaureate program. Special education programs vary, as does the quality of support that schools offer to special-education students as they get into higher grades. If you have a child with special needs, visit a classroom, talk with a counselor, and interview the teachers. Choose a setting with the necessary flexibility or structure to help your child succeed.

Community relationship. One school district with a rural his-tory experienced rapid growth when empty land was transformed into multiple subdivisions. New schools were overenrolled before they opened their doors. So the district went to the people for a big-ger bite of the tax base. In the new subdivisions, voters passed the measure, but the rural voters wanted nothing to do with it, and they were a majority.

A query at the local library reference desk can yield newspaper articles that give you an idea of the relationship between the commu-nity and education. Experienced real estate agents can give subjective impressions about attitudes toward education in certain areas.

Reputation and experience. After parental influence, study after study shows the greatest determinant of a child's success is the class-room teacher. Good teachers recognize when something is not going well and take action. The seventh-grade teachers at one middle school

---

Added Value

Enrichment programs that stimulate your child's interests in learning are wonderful—when they are the right match for your child's interests and needs. But a great teacher in a regular classroom can also challenge stu-dents in creative ways. An eighth-grade social studies teacher routinely taught students about the judicial system by staging a mock trial of a crimi-nal case. Students took on roles of attorneys and witnesses and even the judge. Kids got hooked and joined the mock trial team in high school. Many went on from there to careers in law-related fields. A dedicated teacher pointed them in a direction they might not otherwise have discovered.

decided Andrew was bright but lazy; he just didn't want to do the work. They were not interested in the medical opinions that he had a pervasive developmental disorder affecting how he functioned in school. In the same school, though, eighth-grade teachers called his mother and welcomed her to come in and talk about her son, who was already struggling by the second week of school. The teachers, rather than the school or the program, made the difference and helped this student have a successful year.

Sometimes it takes only one teacher to capture a child's academic interests—or smash them. "Mr. Anderson is so funny!" Kathy grins just thinking about her third-grade teacher.

"Mrs. Childress is my favorite teacher of my whole life!" Hillary's eyes glow when she explains why she likes Mrs. Childress so much.

"I hate Mrs. Smith. She's mean." Jeff crosses his arms and scowls.

Don't discount the opinions of children just because they're only eight years old. They may be one of the most candid sources of information you'll come across.

Some schools brusquely discourage inquiries about choosing a particular teacher. Others welcome them. Since so much depends on the classroom teacher from year to year, it's worth investigating whether your school, public or private, will allow parental input into matching teachers and students.

Experiences of other parents may well be your first introduction to a new option. Don and his wife, Adrian, were considering homeschooling their three children. Several of their friends were homeschooling, and after observing their success, Don and Adrian decided to try it with their own kids.

Inspect the building. No matter what kind of school you close in on, make a personal visit and see with your own eyes what the environment will be like for your child.

The principal of an elementary school showed parents around the school. He waved his hands toward the walls that did not go all the way to the ceiling. "The school was built with an open construction plan," he explained, "so kids could move easily from one area to another." The problem, though, was that the educational theory behind the open construction had gone out of vogue, and now the school had no money to close up the classrooms. Noise drifting over the open walls from one class to another was a steady challenge.

Walk around the building. Make sure the noise level is not an obstacle to learning, particularly if your child is sensitive. Check out how easy it is to find and get to the restrooms or outside doors. Take note of any visible safety issues inside the building or on the playground, or in the way traffic flows around the school at busy times.

Notice the walls as you walk down the hall. Student work on display should represent all abilities, not just the A students. What is the library like? Do all the classrooms have computers?

Meet the principal. Satisfy yourself that you're comfortable with the principal's philosophy and attention. Susan's son has an unusual developmental disorder. When he enrolled in kindergarten, the principal essentially patted her hand and said, "Don't worry, we know what we're doing." She barely listened to anything Susan said. Susan was prepared for educators not to be familiar with her son's disorder, because it was rare. She hoped only to find a principal who was open to learning about it. Nine years later, when it was time for high school, Susan visited the high school principal. She left relieved that the administrator did in fact understand her son's issues and had an up-to-date philosophy of education that was seeping down through the ranks and into the classrooms.

During a visit with a principal, ask questions about clear expectations for teachers, how teachers work together, and keeping good teachers at the school. Listen for answers that are fresh and specific, not canned and general. For instance, one principal might say he observes the teachers in their classrooms when he has time, while another has a specific plan to visit every teacher's room once each semester. One principal might say she encourages teachers to work together in teams, while another says that each teacher is assigned to a specific task force that meets once a month.

Visit a classroom. Always visit a classroom while children are present. Judge for yourself whether the environment is a place where your child can thrive. Make sure it has the structure or flexibility that your child needs. Keep your eyes open to see if the teacher has enough support from aides or parent volunteers. Listen to hear whether the teacher gives praise and encouragement or shouts across the room at students who are off task. Look for areas in the classroom where a child can go to calm down and regroup after being upset or just to do something quiet and alone.

Pop your head into more than one class. You don't have to stay a long time. Visiting several rooms will give you an idea whether the school as a whole has a tone conducive to learning or whether you'll want to avoid certain teachers. Stick around for lunchtime and observe how school staff interacts with children in the cafeteria or on the playground. Are they modeling the values you want your child to learn for problem solving and respect of others?

Homeschool Options

"I could never homeschool," Nancy says. "I already have trouble getting him to do things. I don't want my relationship with my son to be like that."

Diedra says, "You must look at yourself and know if you have the guts to stick it out and make the child do the work in a loving way." Diedra and her daughter loved homeschooling. But Debbie knows it's not for everyone. "Each child is so different, and parents need to look at their child's temperament before doing what we did."

If you think homeschooling is right for your child and your family, you don't have to compare district statistics or interview the principal—that's you! But even within the world of homeschooling, you have options.

Once you understand state graduation requirements and state standards, you can develop your own curriculum. Some ambitious parents find this a delightful challenge. Others would lose their minds. Many homeschooling families purchase a packaged curriculum that takes them through the grades in a consistent way and ensures that they meet state standards.

More and more public schools welcome a partnership with homeschoolers. With dual enrollment, your child can participate in music, sports, clubs, or other group activities. Your child can attend classes for only certain subjects, relieving you of the anxiety of teaching outside your strengths.

Often in homeschool networks, parents swap teaching subjects to make the most of everyone's strengths and interests. If you choose to connect with a group like this, be thinking about what you can contribute. Can you teach a writing class if someone else will handle science for your children? If you're looking for a network to join, call several churches and ask about connecting with other homeschoolers. One contact will lead to another and you'll soon find yourself part of a welcoming community.

A final option for homeschooling is to enroll your child in an online school district. This school may be across the state, hundreds of miles away. The district provides the curriculum and specific lesson assignments and assessments. Dan's family used this option for an adopted child with emotional disturbances that made it impossible for her to function well in a conventional classroom, but many normally adjusted children enjoy it also.

It All Comes Down to You

As you investigate education options, you'll see features that fascinate you but are not essential. Others become increasingly important as you go through the selection process. A few are downright essential, and you won't choose a school without them. These perceptions determine the weight of various features.

Narrow your list and compare the weight of the features schools offer. Be aware that your first choice might not work out; a long wait- ing list might stack the odds against you, or school administrators may decide your child and the school are not a match. Be sure you have a second choice you are also enthusiastic about. And don't for- get your child's input. Even a young child will show nonverbal response to the environment. Older children can tell you what they want or don't want, what they like or don't like. You might decide that the public school around the corner is a great choice.

Start well in advance of the day your child will start school. Ask specifically about deadlines for applications or choice permits. Hang on to the information you uncover during the choice process, and keep your research fresh. If you need to make a change for some rea- son, you won't have to start all over again.

In the end, you want a school that your child is eager and ener- gized to attend, teachers who understand and appreciate your child's strengths, teaching methods consistent with your values, and a level of influence with principals and teachers you're comfortable with when it comes to making decisions about your child.

CHAPTER

8

Your Personalized
School Checklist

(photocopy one set for each child and for each school)

My Family's Non-negotiables

What education priorities do you have for your child?

_____

_____

_____

Finish these five sentences to help you define them:
The most important thing for my child's education is . . .

_____

_____

Above all, I want my child to have . . .

_____

_____

My child needs _____ to be successful . . .

_____

_____

My child learns best when . . .

_____

_____

The perfect school for my child would emphasize . . .

_____

_____

Spiritual Non-negotiables

Use this grid to help you determine the importance and priorities of these faith basics for:

1. Prayer—I want my child to be taught prayer at school.
   very important   moderately important   not important

2. The Bible—I want my child to learn Bible curriculum at school.
   very important   moderately important   not important

3. Worldview—I want my child protected from unbiblical teachings while at school.
   very important   moderately important   not important

4. Role models—I want my child to have Christian role models at school.
   very important   moderately important   not important

5. Peers—I want to increase the chances that my children's peers will be a positive influence.
   very important   moderately important   not important

General Factors Checklist

Name of School _____

My Overall Rating of this School (1-10) _____

Is mid-year enrollment an option?   yes   no

What is the school's philosophy of education?

_____

_____

What are the school's primary goals?

_____

_____

Does the school have a psychologist on staff?   yes   no

Does the school have a full-time nurse?   yes   no

Does the school have a speech specialist?   yes   no

Does the school have a librarian?   yes   no

Does the school have a curriculum specialist?   yes   no

Does the school have a special-ed program?   yes   no

Does the school have a gifted program?   yes   no

What is the actual average class size?   _____

What is the maximum class size?   _____

What is the student/teacher ratio?   _____

What is the male/female staff ratio?   _____

Describe the calendar year—traditional or year round?

_____

What is the total number of school days? _____

What are the school's hours? _____

Is there staggered dismissal?   yes   no

Is summer school available?   yes   no

Is there after-school, on-site childcare?   yes   no

Are there school-sponsored after-school activities?   yes   no

Are there aides in the classroom?   yes   no

If so, what are their qualifications?

_____

_____

Circle all the transportation options available:
    school bus, carpool, city bus, parking for students

Circle all the cafeteria options:
    hot lunch, cold lunch, microwaves available for students, vend-
    ing machines, beverages for sale, hot breakfast served, reduced
    price lunch for qualified students

Is this a nonsmoking campus?   yes   no

Describe the parental visitation policy—drop in? by appointment?
    check in at office?

_____

If there are fund-raisers, are they required?   yes   no

How many fund-raisers are there a year? _____

What is expected of parents for classroom help? Circle all that
    apply: field trips, fund-raising, supervision on playground,
    lunch supervision, parking lot management, library help, paper
    grading, party planning, other _____

How often are parent-teacher conferences? _____

How does the "feeder" system work with this school?

_____

Is there vocational/career counseling available at the
    secondary level?   yes   no
I can get my child to this school and home again.   yes   no
Circle all the programs that this school offers: band, orchestra,
    choir, drama, sports, forensics, cheerleading, science enrichment,
    foreign language enrichment, Bible clubs, _____,

    _____, _____.

Ask for and attach copies of the school's test scores or any other
objective measures to evaluate the performance and improvement
of the students.

NOTES:

Curriculum Checklist

Name of School _____

My Overall Curriculum Rating (1-10) _____

The overall curriculum will meet my child's basic academic needs.	yes	no
I am able to fill in or enhance the curriculum where I feel it is lacking.	yes	no
I have seen the textbooks my child will be using at this school and have written down the titles.	yes	no
I have written down the titles of any books my child will be assigned in addition to textbooks.	yes	no
After doing some research, I am confident that the material presented through the curriculum is not harmful to my child.	yes	no
If I have concerns about the curriculum, I feel confident the principal and staff of the school will work with me to make sure nothing in the curriculum will damage or hurt my child in any way.	yes	no
If my child uses this curriculum, it will not interfere with his/her Christian faith.	yes	no
If my child uses this school's curriculum, it has the potential to build his/her Christian faith.	yes	no
The curriculum and the way it will be presented in class will match my child's learning style.	yes	no

I have gone the extra mile and called school board
    members, done a newspaper search at the library,
    and talked to friends to find out if there is a
    history of the school providing questionable
    or anti-biblical curriculum.   yes   no

There is curriculum or special materials available
    for gifted students.   yes   no

The special-ed material will meet my child's needs.   yes   no

There is adequate curriculum on second languages.   yes   no

There are up-to-date computers, and part of my
    child's instruction will take place via computer.   yes   no

I know about the sex education curriculum and
    I am comfortable with my child participating.   yes   no

NOTES:

Building Checklist

Name of School _____

My Overall Building Rating (1-10) _____

The overall atmosphere is cheerful and inviting.	yes	no
The school is clean.	yes	no
There is enough lighting in the parking lot.	yes	no
The parking lot is safe to enter and exit traffic.	yes	no
The drop-off area is safe; I am not afraid my child will be in danger of traffic.	yes	no
Safety check: During the school day, the school building is locked, except for observed entrances.	yes	no
The lighting inside the school is adequate.	yes	no
The classrooms are quiet; excess noise is eliminated.	yes	no
The bathrooms are clean.	yes	no
The desks, tables, chairs meet or exceed my expectations.	yes	no
I have noted the recreation/physical education surfaces: grass, dirt, sand, asphalt, concrete, bark or wood chips, and they are satisfactory.	yes	no
The playground equipment is inviting and safe.	yes	no
The school has a gym for indoor sports, and it is adequate.	yes	no
The school's band room or music room will meet my child's needs.	yes	no

The library is complete and will meet my child's
needs.   yes   no

The lunchroom is clean and pleasant.   yes   no

Lockers are provided.   yes   no

For safety's sake, during the school day visitors
will be monitored.   yes   no

NOTES:

_____

_____

_____

_____

_____

_____

_____

_____

_____

_____

_____

_____

_____

_____

_____

_____

_____

Staff Checklist

Name of School: _____

My Overall Rating for the Staff (1-10) _____

Are the teachers credentialed?   yes   no

If the teachers are not credentialed, what training does the school
    require? _____

Are the teachers required to keep up with teacher in-services and/or
    continue their education?   yes   no

If a teacher is performing poorly, does the school have the authority
    to fire the teacher? Explain the school's policy on teacher retention:

_____

_____

_____

_____

_____

I believe this staff of teachers can motivate my child. yes   no

Sample questions for teachers:
(Good answers will be specific, clear, and measurable. Beware of
vague answers such as, "We evaluate as we go" or "We'll cross that
bridge when we come to it.")

My main education goal for my child is _____.
    How can you help me achieve that goal?

My child's primary learning style is _____.
How will you be able to use this strength to help my child
learn?

How will you show appreciation for my child's strengths and
abilities?

What strengths do you have personally that will help motivate my
child to learn and/or succeed in this school?

Tell me about a time that you helped a child overcome a learning
obstacle and succeed.

Tell me about the expectations you'll have for my child.

If my child performs above grade level academically, what will you
do to enhance his/her learning experience?

Tell me about how you best communicate with parents.

What are your expectations for me?

What personal teaching goals do you have for this year?

How often will you assess my child's progress?

My questions:

_____

_____

_____

_____

_____

_____

_____

_____

_____

Sample questions for the principal:

(Good answers will be specific, clear, and measurable. If the answers are part of a written policy, that's good, too. You want answers that show the school has accountability, strategy, and vision.)

If my child's learning pace is faster or slower than the class, what can the school do to help him/her to get the best education possible?

Tell me about a problem you identified last year and how you solved it.

Why did you choose the instruction methods this school uses?

How do you communicate performance expectations for teachers?

How do you monitor the teachers' performances?

What professional development do you offer to teachers to make sure they meet the school's goals and expectations?

If I have a problem with a teacher, the curriculum, or another issue, how would you like me to handle that?

How can I know that my child will be safe at this school?

How do you get and keep great teachers?

My questions:

_____

_____

_____

_____

_____

_____

Behavior Management Checklist

Name of School _____

My Overall Behavior Management Rating (1-10) _____

Is the teacher the primary disciplinarian?   yes   no

To what extent are students expected to monitor one another?

_____

_____

Are problem-solving strategies provided to students? Is training
mandatory or voluntary?

_____

_____

To what extent is making restitution a part of the discipline
procedures?

_____

_____

When is the teacher allowed to make a referral to director/principal?

_____

_____

Are students ever isolated as a form of discipline?

_____

_____

What are the suspension policies?

_____

_____

Are students ever given time-outs or held in from recess? If you
want your child to always be allowed to have recess, is this an
option?

_____

_____

If corporal punishment is used, are you comfortable with the procedures and policies of the school?

_____

_____

Is there a "no tolerance" policy at the school? If so, is it reasonable?

_____

_____

NOTES:

_____

_____

_____

_____

_____

_____

Private School Checklist

Name of School _____

My Overall Rating of this School (1-10) _____

Is the school accredited?   yes   no

What is the total enrollment? _____

Is the school at full enrollment? If not, at what percentage capacity
     is it filled?_____

What is director/principal's background?

_____

_____

_____

Is there a director of admissions?   yes   no

Is there a waiting list?   yes   no

Are siblings given priority for admission?   yes   no

Is the school coeducational or single gender? _____

If religious, is the school affiliated? If so, with what organization?

_____

_____

_____

Is it a non-profit school?   yes   no

Is it owned by a corporation?   yes   no

Is it privately owned?   yes   no

Is there a board of directors? If so, who is on the board and what are their qualifications?

_____

_____

_____

What is the cost of tuition? _____

Are there scholarships available? If so, what are the criteria?

_____

_____

_____

What is the payment schedule? _____

Is there an application fee? If so, what is it? _____

What is the enrollment deadline? _____

Is there automatic enrollment for continuing students or must students reapply when moving to middle school or high school?

_____

_____

_____

What is involved in the application process?

_____

_____

_____

_____

What assessments will my child need?

_____

_____

_____

What is the retention policy?

_____

What are the academic standards for my child?

_____

_____

_____

What are the social/emotional development standards for my child?

_____

_____

_____

_____

_____

_____

_____

Homeschool Checklist

I have the time to homeschool.	yes	no
I have the financial resources to homeschool.	yes	no
It is legal in my state to homeschool, and I know where to find out the requirements for homeschooling my child.	yes	no
I have virtual schools available to me through the public schools if I need them.	yes	no
I have researched private cottage schools and homeschool support groups.	yes	no
I am confident my child will receive a great education at home.	yes	no
My spouse supports the goal to homeschool our child/children.	yes	no
I am willing and able to drive my child to extra-curricular activities.	yes	no
I have emotional support through friends and family members that will help me homeschool.	yes	no

Things I need to do to begin a homeschool program for my children are

_____

_____

_____

_____

_____

Homeschool notes continued:

_____

_____

_____

_____

_____

_____

_____

_____

_____

_____

_____

_____

_____

_____

_____

_____

_____

_____

_____

_____

_____

_____

_____

What's Next?

9

The Parent as the Ultimate Teacher

by Charles W. Johnson

If a child is to keep alive his inborn sense of wonder,
he needs the companionship of at least one adult
who can share it, rediscovering with him the joy,
excitement and mystery of the world we live in.
—RACHEL CARSON

My son, if your heart is wise,
then my heart will be glad;
my inmost being will rejoice
when your lips speak what is right.
—PROVERBS 23:15-16

When the film *The Lion, the Witch, and the Wardrobe* was released, my children (now 26 and 22) quickly found time to view it. As enjoyable as that experience was, they told me, "It didn't compare to the memories of Dad reading through the entire Chronicles of Narnia aloud with voices and accents no less." Now, I know that Liam Neeson's Aslan was a far more impressive rendition than my own, but the joy of sharing C. S. Lewis's story and his language with my children has lasted for more than a decade—for my son, my daughter, and me.

As a former school principal and a parent, I saw similar situations in many families as parents connected with their children in their learning pursuits. Regardless of the educational choices that parents make for their children, one factor remains true: The parent serves as the first and primary teacher for the child. No other adult has the opportunity to instill a love of learning, to monitor the child's development from day one through the terrible twos to that first day of formal education, and on through the traumas of middle school and the potentially turbulent waters of the teens. Consequently, parents possess lifelong chances to guide and direct through interaction and involvement in whatever school setting the family selects.

Before They Go to School

This role begins long before any formal education occurs, when the mother sings those rhyming lullabies and the father responds to the first of countless "why?" questions. A love of reading can be built (and indeed needs to be developed) before the first book report is assigned. When a parent reads to a child, she builds a bond of connection and creates the desire to find out what happens next in the story. As with our reading of Narnia, the love of language and the delight of narrative create fundamental building blocks in developing academic success. Even during the toddler years, parents can ignite the desire to learn and to build problem-solving skills as they engage their little ones in becoming curious about nature, in learning about animals, and in watching seedlings grow into sturdy plants.

In addition, as parents we cannot overlook the knowledge that habits are caught as much as they are taught. Now that my children have completed their college education, I am amazed to see them both involved in the educational field. Even though I left the schools to pursue other ventures, my daughter, now a teacher of fifth graders, remembers her childhood days when I would bring home schoolwork and tell stories about student adventures. Believe it or not, it made her want to consider teaching as an occupation. She recalls my efforts to develop a creative approach that would ensure my students' understanding of a piece of literature, and both of our children reflect our love of reading. Your child will model his attitude toward learning and all aspects of education after the example that he sees in his parents. If mothers and fathers spend their time watching television rather than reading books, chances are good that the children will identify entertainment with that passive approach rather than engaging their imaginations with reading. On the other hand, if the parent exhibits a love of learning, showing his or her own curiosity and excitement about how things work and how they can be understood, the child is also more likely to dig in to discover and find out the truth about the world around him.

The Schooling Process Begins

Once formal schooling begins, parents must remain actively involved, not delegating all teaching responsibilities, but rather partnering with school personnel to ensure that academic work is understood and in line with the principles instilled in the home. This effort provides the framework for the child to understand the continuum between home and school—not the great divide that so often makes it seem that they are two distinct worlds.

Throughout the child's educational career, parents play a variety of roles: tutor, cheerleader, project manager, coach, motivator, processor, springboard, and sounding board. Beginning with the initial selection of the school environment, mothers and fathers need to communicate closely and continually with the school leadership: the classroom teacher, the school counselor, and the administrators. Make the effort to clarify and understand behavioral and academic expectations before classes begin and maintain the communication channels all the time the child is in school. You cannot assume that everything is fine just because the teacher has not sent home a warning notice. In some schools such notification is mandated only in case of below-average grades, but teachers' busyness and the numbers of students they deal with may not make ongoing communication of progress a high priority regarding the students who are simply getting by.

At the same time, the parent should monitor the child at home, asking about class instruction, ensuring that homework is completed, and checking to see not only that assignments are finished but that they are also understood. Depending on the school choice that has been made, you also have the responsibility to process the class content through the context of a biblical worldview, particularly in science and history classes but also in literature at the middle- and high-school levels. One common danger occurs when parents assume that just because a student attends a classical school or even a Christian one, all of the content is in accordance with the principles and outlook of the home front. Parents should always review what is taught, supplementing and explaining the significant factors in developing a Christian worldview.

No school is perfect, and the parent is responsible for filling in the gaps. For example, most public schools do not have a curriculum for teaching Bible. (Although some may have a Bible as Literature course, such a class cannot by its very nature encourage personal study of the Word of God in a devotional sense.) As a result, Bible study is an area that would fall primarily into the parental purview. Depending on the grade level of the student and the experience and knowledge of the parent, many homeschooling situations eventually encounter gaps in the available academic coverage. We homeschooled our children for several years, but we sought out group settings for instruction in particular areas, including lab science and foreign language.

While parents need to be available and accessible in helping their children understand their classes in school, they cross a line when they do too much of the student's work. The school district in which

I worked was characterized by high expectations and parental support, but sometimes that assistance went too far. Whether it was the fourth-grade California missions presentation or just ongoing homework assignments, the teachers often had suspicions about the maturity of what was turned in. In fact, the middle school principal recognized the realities behind the parents' desire for accomplishment and face-tiously said, "Why don't we just be honest about the whole thing and announce that the annual science project contest is open only to parents of sixth graders? No students need to apply." This situation occurs when parents no longer act as teachers. Just as effective educators direct and guide their students into a comprehension of the subject matter, parents should take the same approach through questioning and monitoring instead of completing the work on the students' behalf.

And that leads the parent into the combined role of serving as both the coach and the cheerleader of the child's schooling. Children need motivation and affirmation, particularly as they set out on new ventures. As a parent, you know your child better than any other adult does, and you recognize when he or she needs that gentle soothing of encouragement. In addition, you know when the child's need is not for compassion but for deliberate challenge, urging, and driving toward hard work to master a concept.

Teachers in the classroom can do only so much; they need the support and cooperation of the parent at home to build their students' success. During my time as a school counselor, I once felt frustrated when a parent told a teacher, "It was my child's responsibility to complete his homework. I didn't feel that I needed to hang all over him to make sure it was done." The teacher who received that comment was trying her hardest to keep the parent informed, but in her mind, the student was skating through with the same level of responsibility shown by the parent. As a result, the student was failing to perform, and the teacher felt she was the only one feeling concerned.

Beyond a certain stage (middle school or beyond, depending on the track record of the student), parents definitely can—and should—back out of too tight an oversight of the student's work, but that doesn't mean that the communication should stop. Parents should be aware of assignments, upcoming tests, research papers, as a means to track the student's progress. Some young people need that gentle nudge and assurance that they can manage to comprehend and complete the work, while others need the accountability of firmer supervision.

The School Connection

While this chapter thus far has focused on the parent's interaction with the child in the school setting, how can you exhibit true involvement in the school itself? Most schools, whether public or Christian, have some sort of parent-teacher association, organization, or fellowship, and as the homeschooling movement has grown, networks of homeschooling families have also developed as a means of providing mutual support and encouragement. Few parents need additional meetings to complicate their lives, but knowledgeable moms and dads realize that connection with associations like these can also serve as a reinforcement of their child's link to the school community. By engaging with other parents, you can become aware of issues facing the school administration.

One school superintendent encountered a sensitive curricular issue, and he turned to the PTA leadership for input and insight in dealing with the challenge. "These parents were the ones who had invested in the best interests of the school and the district," he said. That superintendent was more inclined to listen to involved parents because they had been supportive. He is wary of "single-issue-parents" because he doesn't know them and he isn't sure they understand the climate of the school.

Volunteer and help the teacher. Parental involvement can include investment of many hours or few, from regular assistance in your child's classroom in the lower grades to willingness to serve as a chaperone on a field trip. As long as the parent approaches the opportunities under appropriate submission to the teacher's rules and processes (rather than seeking to correct or control the situation), most teachers will gratefully welcome the aid. After all, corralling 19 kindergartners for a trip to the local zoo requires multiple adults (all with the patience of Job and the reach of an octopus).

In the primary grades, teachers will often appreciate the assistance offered by parents who are willing to serve as reading guides or simply as listeners to youngsters as the children learn to read. Some may be open to parents' help during story time; if moms or dads with a more dramatic flair read children's books to the class, this would allow the educators to do additional planning or simply to be out of the spotlight for a short time. Parents do not necessarily need a science background to assist the teachers by participating in classroom experiments, and other teachers may accept parental help in reviewing math facts with small groups.

In all of these situations, the key to being a helpful parent lies in accepting direction from the teacher. By being cooperative in such a volunteer role, the parent can both assist the instructor and monitor what is going on in the classroom. You can observe the teacher's style and content, gleaning methods to help your own child, and you can also discreetly watch how your student interacts with his classmates. These opportunities should not be seen as chances to spy on the teacher or to gather evidence against a particular instructor. At the same time, through offering classroom support, the parent can gain access and relationship with the educator, opening conversational doors that can produce dividends beyond your child's improved performance.

Depending on the school format, classroom volunteerism need not stop in the primary grades. As your child matures, teachers in higher grades may also accept a helping hand, whether you serve as a one-on-one tutor or as a driver to that anticipated field trip to the Museum of Natural History. By going along on such a venture, parents can hear what your children hear, providing valuable insight as you debrief with your student later. If the museum docent takes off on an evolutionary slant, the thoughtful parent can develop the response to help the child process what he's being presented—a response from the biblical viewpoint.

For the homeschooling parent, these classroom and school connections may occur in the context of shared experiences with other families. While the parents are carrying the primary instructional load, communication with others can provide chances to go with your strengths. Maybe you are fluent in Spanish but feeble in science. Find another family with abilities in the area you need and needs in the area you are able. The growth of the homeschooling movement has opened up the possibilities for shared expertise and enabled moms and dads to avoid the isolation that was often a part of its early history.

Volunteer and help the school community

Involvement with the school itself, however, is not limited to the classroom. Effective, community-oriented school systems promote parent participation, and as the public demands ever greater school accountability, parents can find numerous opportunities to provide direction for the schools. This is not only true in charter schools, many of which are governed by parent boards, but also in other schools, both public and private. Curricular committees, school improvement efforts, and other advisory opportunities provide guidance in the way the schools are going.

Before a book is purchased for a school library, many districts ask a committee formed from the general public to review it page by page. Sometimes the members of the school board assume this responsibility, but they may have the option of delegating the reading to a local committee. To ensure that a responsible parent's outlook is considered in the book selection, why not volunteer to assist in reading and approving the books your youngster may find on the shelves at school?

Schools often include parents in advisory committees like the School Improvement Program, which designates budgeted dollars toward particular purchases to benefit the students. Again, parents who volunteer to participate in such a committee should do so with an attitude that lends itself toward peacemaking. In this way, moms and dads can illustrate a point of view that takes the best interests of the entire school into account.

Show up at important events
Another way to show ongoing support for the school and also for your child is by carving out the time to attend events. Whether or not your child is involved in athletics, music, drama, or art, make the commitment to be present at those games, concerts, or performances. All too often, only the parents of the participants attend, but showing up at a cross-country meet or a sixth-grade band recital, even if your child is not a part, can provide a great vote of confidence to the coach, the music teacher, and the other parents. These opportunities for activities may also be open to homeschooled students, so if families choose that particular route, they should not assume that doors to athletics or other activities are closed to their children. Ask the question, and if the answer comes back negative, pursue it further by asking, "Why can my child *not* participate?"

Make it a point to attend back-to-school nights and open houses, as well. Often the attendance at these events declines after the elementary grades when youngsters no longer ask their parents to see their class work. But these evenings become even more important in the middle- and high-school levels. They are designed to inform parents about the curriculum, behavioral expectations, and accomplishments of the class. The teachers have already put in a full day of teaching, so if few parents come to an evening open house, the instructors can feel defeated with a sense of "what's the use?" On the other hand, a good crowd can affirm the educator and help him realize that his efforts are, in fact, appreciated and his partnership with the parents is valuable.

One high school teacher commented, "It was on those [back-to-school] nights that I could tell which parents were going to be my allies in the upcoming year. I carefully planned my presentation to ensure that those who attended would have a clear view of our curriculum, the homework, and testing expectations, but I also had the chance to let them know what I was about and how I wanted to partner with them for the best interests of their children."

Help with extracurricular activities
Besides extracurricular activities that are sponsored by the school, many other opportunities provide outings for your young people, and they too can use adult participation. In many instances, ministries like Young Life, the Fellowship of Christian Athletes, and Campus Life have a positive impact on school campuses across the nation, but they often meet in the homes of the participants. Could you volunteer your house and bake up a few dozen cookies for refreshments? Some parents may even choose to serve as volunteer leaders in these organizations, leading Bible studies and fostering discipleship in those students who want to know more about the Christian life.

While committee meetings, attendance at activities and evening programs, and even school-related ministry opportunities are valuable time commitments, praying for the school, its teachers, students, and staff members serves a vital role. Such a connection contributes to the overall school atmosphere, and it can show other parents and students where you stand spiritually. Many parents find that organizations such as Moms in Touch help them find support. In every grade level, whether through homeschool, Christian schools, or other private institutions, charter schools, or traditional public schools, your prayers can make a difference for the faculty and students.

So What Happens at Home?

Parental involvement in your child's education does not take place only on the school campus or at activities. For the greatest success, it must also continue on the home front. After all, you are the most significant and knowledgeable teacher in your child's life. You are the one who must understand and respond to his or her individual needs. You recognize when to supply encouragement and when to provide discipline to ensure that the child achieves the success of which he is capable.

Parents should fully explore and reinforce the learning style of the particular child. Some children are auditory, some visual, some kinesthetic; some can concentrate in the midst of all kinds of distraction while others need relative silence (or at least minimal interruptions); some function best right after school and others need some recreation or a breather before buckling down to homework; and some may need healthy snacks or drinks nearby to tackle successfully what is before them. For more information on learning styles and how best to incorporate and utilize them, see chapter 6.

Time management

Perhaps the most important gift a parent can give a child is the development of a sound and effective time management system. For most children (and far too many adults), the skills of prioritizing tasks and understanding the sequencing of responsibilities must be practiced and guided by an adult. As a loving parent, you have the awesome privilege and the responsibility to assist your child in developing those skills, and schoolwork can provide the training ground. Go beyond asking your child what his assignments are, and assist him in breaking them down into manageable tasks and in setting a plan to attack them. By doing so, you are building life skills that will serve him well into adulthood.

Although far too many young people echo the familiar catch-phrase, "I work best under pressure," the reality is that few actually do so. Planning ahead and biting off smaller portions of larger tasks allows for more effective processing of information than does the last-minute cramming approach. In addition, such an effort can build in some cushion against the inevitable interruptions and last-minute stresses.

Remember that time management goes far beyond schoolwork: It encompasses all aspects of your child's life. All work and no play can indeed create a one-dimensional young person who may be successful in classroom performance but lacking in social skills. Encourage your son or daughter to become involved in selected school activities, whether they be sports, drama, art, journalism, or campus clubs. The connections formed through extracurricular programs can provide motivation and additional interest in what's going on at the campus. Sometimes these efforts can give needed spark about school in general.

One school counselor recalls a student who struggled with classroom performance. "His parents chose to take him out of his athletic endeavors, hoping that the additional time without athletic commitment would be beneficial toward his academics. In effect, the opposite occurred. Without the structure of practice every afternoon, the young man was like a boat without a rudder. After he'd missed the first part of the season, his grades were wallowing; however, he was still eligible to compete, and when they talked the coach into letting him practice with the team, the restoration provided just the jump start that he needed, and his grades climbed. As he experienced success on the athletic field, that accomplishment spurred him on to corresponding success in his classes."

At the same time, parents need to monitor the time spent in extracurricular activities. After all, they are *extra*. So many opportunities exist for young people today that it's easy to let activities and the tight scheduling overwhelm the necessity for the class work. Some may become so enthralled with the busyness that they lose sight of the academic realities. Because you know your own child, discuss which two or three activities he or she would like to commit to and then support the decision, carefully watching the time invested.

Monitoring friendships

Along with activities, sports, and clubs, parents can also benefit by assessing and monitoring the group of friends with whom your child associates. Encourage your youngster to invite them over, and by meeting and getting to know them, you can recognize the ones who have a positive influence on your son or daughter. Research abounds with the influence that peers have over youngsters and teens, so parents need to seize the opportunity to observe the group dynamics and friends' personalities, encouraging relationships with those who tend to spur positive accomplishments from your child.

But while fellow children and teens influence how your own son or daughter may act, never lose sight of the enormous opportunity you have as a parent. While peers may affect momentary decisions, parents are in a position to influence long-range attitudes and performance through modeling and encouragement. And you, Mom and Dad, have the chance to be your child's ultimate teacher. As important as academic performance may be, by whatever course your family chooses to take, realize that your sons' and daughters' true education extends beyond the classroom walls. Through your involvement in the educational process and with God's gracious guidance, you can teach them not only how to learn, but how to live.

Equipping Your Child for Lifelong Learning and Success

by Cheri Fuller

The aim of education is the knowledge
not of fact, but of values.
—DEAN WILLIAM R. INGE

Train a child in the way he should go, and
when he is old he will not turn from it.
—PROVERBS 22:6

The MacKenzie family moved around a lot. They homeschooled during the seven years the parents served as missionaries overseas, and they eventually moved to Oklahoma after a short stint in another state where their children attended a Christian school. Soon after entering the public middle school in their community, their son Anthony went into a downward spiral. He'd scored very low on standardized tests taken on enrollment day, and after a week or two, he was so discouraged with his low test scores and mounds of homework, he wanted to quit.

Anthony's mom, Maggie, began volunteering in his classroom one afternoon a week. There she realized more clearly the challenges and expectations for sixth graders. The teacher gave her supplemental materials for Anthony, and she began working with him after school at home—having him reading his science and history textbooks aloud; providing extra books, maps, and atlases from the library to enrich the material; and equipping him with study strategies.

When the students were to enter the science fair, Anthony found a project that piqued his curiosity; his mom, dad, and brothers helped him find interesting resources and cheered him on as he worked. When he was awarded first place in his division, Anthony, who'd always been in the shadow of his two high-achieving older siblings, began to feel more confident. After that success, he made it a goal to get straight A's and worked even harder. During the many months Anthony persevered, his parents focused on his progress and effort, instead of on what he hadn't yet achieved or an occasional low grade.

It wasn't easy and Anthony had plenty of setbacks, but with his optimism, effort, and determination fueling him, by the end of the *next* year, he'd made all A's for the first time ever, and his standardized test scores went way up.

This young man didn't stop there. Though he had to work harder than other classmates to get high grades, by college he was a 4.0 student and was on the president's honor roll. Along the way, the boy who struggled with middle-school homework fell in love with learning, which took him to a Japanese university to teach English as a second language and on a history fellowship to tour and write of his travels in Europe and around the world. Now in his late 20s, this lifelong learner plans to study for a Ph.D. and become a college professor.

Just as Anthony's parents found, there are many ways you can equip your child for lifelong learning and success. This chapter will share how you can be a homework consultant and encourager yet leave the ownership of the responsibility with your child. You'll also learn how your role model as a parent is one of the best ways to impact your child's achievement. In addition, you'll see how a positive home environment that supports learning and develops strong character and values is vital as you build momentum for lifelong learning.

What's Your Role in Homework?

When I was a classroom teacher, it wasn't hard to tell which kids were getting too much outside help from their parents. A project and poster would look like a graphics team had created it, or a homework paper would be perfect, but the student would fail the test on the same material. Today the urge to get overinvolved in homework is just as great, and perhaps even greater because some experts say that many parents "consumed with overprotective zeal" are coddling their kids through homework, correcting their errors or even doing the papers for them.[1] Telltale clues of overinvolvement are when parents say, "*Our* project is taking a lot of time," or "*We* have so much homework tonight!" Actually, it's the child's project and homework, and even though parents are just trying to help, if they take over, kids start thinking, *Why care or put out so much effort? Mom and Dad will do it for me!*

What can you do then to support your children in learning and help them take ownership? The first step is to *build responsibility.* Kids who learn responsibility at home (by doing a few daily, age-appropriate chores and completing their own homework assignments) tend to be more competent and successful at school. You should provide an organized study area (with good light, paper, and color-coded file folders to keep papers in, and let them choose some of their own supplies) because disorganization causes stress and distracts from the learning process. Children need a break and physical play after school, but then you need to establish a fixed place in your house and a regular time for homework and reading because it helps build a strong "mental set" for studying.

Another thing you can do is show your child how to break assignments into doable bites so the pressure won't be on the night before due date (when you're more tempted to pick up the ball and do the project for him so he won't get a zero)—but then expect your child to do the work. Teach good study strategies that build on your child's learning strengths (see chapter 6, "My Child's Learning Style and Best

Learning Environment," for some practical ones)—but let him or her keep the "ownership" of the homework and school responsibilities.

And if he's done a math problem incorrectly, show him how to work a similar problem but let *him* be the one to correct it on his worksheet. When parents repeatedly bail kids out if they fail to do their work, the kids don't learn responsibility or use their own abilities. But when you encourage self-reliance and responsibility, you'll be empowering your child with an "I can do it" kind of attitude.

Boost Your Child's Curiosity and Thinking Skills

As long as kids stay curious, they are motivated to learn, but when their curiosity dies, their learning ability suffers. Many experts believe curiosity may be *the most important factor* for children's brain development and their ability to tackle academic tasks. Just as my friends the MacKenzies found, when their son's curiosity was stimulated, it boosted his motivation to learn.

Like curiosity, thinking is perhaps one of the most important subjects of all, and it begins at home. Use opportunities in real, everyday living to give your kids problem-solving practice. Let them help figure out how far apart to space vegetable and flower seedlings in the garden. Before a trip, let them help plan and budget the vacation money and navigate using maps while en route to your destination. Turn a walk to the park into a nature investigation with an inexpensive magnifying glass, a sack for interesting rocks or leaves, and a critter jar made out of a plastic container with a mesh lid to let in air.

Ask curious questions when you go to the zoo together like "Why do you think this animal has long legs? Is this animal a meat eater or a grass eater?" Give them toothpicks and say, "What are all the ways we can use a toothpick?" Brainstorm and see who can figure out how to use something that would normally be thrown away. "What can we do with a Styrofoam tray the chicken was in?" (After washing, of course!) And there are many other creative ideas kids can think of on their own.

And most of all, take your kids' questions seriously—even though little ones ask a lot of questions that can seem endless. (Remember, this curiosity, these questions, are a *key* to his desire to learn, so avoid putting out the fire!) At the same time, don't feel like you have to give all the answers; it's valuable to help your child think through the question and ask, "What do you think about that?" or "That's a really great question," and then guide him through applying facts he's already learned or coming up with a theory of his own. If you're too busy to talk about it at the time or don't know the answer, write your child's questions on an index card and next time you're at the library, have him take it to the librarian to help discover the answer, or search together on the Internet later.

When kids are in junior high and high school, critical-thinking skills are developing, so it's vital to keep an open dialogue with them about issues and situations they face. When they make a statement that contrasts with your values, avoid overreacting. Instead, guide them through the thought processes, and encourage them to consider what determines right and wrong and to search for what God says about that issue in the Bible. But let your children explain their views and not always be put down for their ideas.

Also, find out what the school is doing to inspire kids' curiosity. If your discoveries prove disappointing, band with other parents to brainstorm for creative ideas and buy hands-on science equipment (lots of which is inexpensive). Meet with teachers and the principal to see how parents can partner to improve the school environment and build students' sense of wonder, curiosity, and motivation for learning.

Build a Home Environment that Supports Learning

We want to have great schools to send our kids to, but the truth is *their home environment has a profound impact on their learning.* The old saying, "The most important work you do takes place within the walls of your home," applies here. Let me demonstrate this truth with an example of how to raise writers (that is, students who have strong writing skills).

When I taught high school English, I could always determine which students did some writing at home with their parents in the course of their everyday life. They did better in classroom writing and generally had a more positive attitude about writing, assuming that it was what grown-ups did in real life, not just cruel and unusual assignments reserved only for school. Then some interesting research came out a few years ago, studying factors in families that support kids' developing writing skills, that confirmed what I'd observed in the classroom.[2]

Here are some of the findings: These children had a lot of conversation and reading at home. There was at least one adult who interacted with them about their writing; took time to let them read their stories, poems, or whatever they'd written aloud; and encouraged them to express themselves on paper. They suggested real reasons to do practical writing like making lists (of friends to invite to a party or foods they'd like to eat in the coming week) and wrote notes to their kids at home on sticky notes, on a whiteboard in a central place for family messages, and in their lunch boxes.

These were not parents who were professional writers, but ones who saw writing as a lifelong skill and encouraged it at home. And writing, by the way, *is* a valuable skill, even (and especially) in this high-tech era. There are well over 30 million jobs today in which people use writing to convey and transfer information; *because* we're in an information-oriented world, success in great part depends on a precise and effective use of spoken and written language. So a young person who can write and speak well (the two skills tend to work together) will be the adult who can rise to the top of his field.

Take this same principle and apply it to other things your children need to learn, such as math (the attitude about math that kids come into the classroom with, and experiences at home with measuring, learning to set up a simple budget, counting toys while putting them away on shelves) and reading (avid young readers tend to come from homes where there's a lot of reading aloud, parents are engaged in their own reading, and interesting books and magazines are available). Not just moms, but *dads* also have an important role in developing their kids to be lifelong learners. Mothers are often the ones expected to help with homework and volunteer at school, but over and over studies show that a *father's* encouragement and support—whether it's reading aloud to his children, sharing a hobby, or showing genuine interest in the content that his kids are learning, not just the grades—can have a powerful impact on raising lifelong learners.

And if you decrease your own and your children's time in front of the television during the school week and spend the time in other, more productive ways like playing board games or talking around the dinner table, you'll be surprised at how this translates into more motivation for learning in the classroom. Excessive TV watching (including DVDs and videotapes) robs kids of important parent-child time and is strongly related to inattention and childhood obesity. And please don't put a television or computer in your young child's room, isolating him or her from family interaction and parental supervision.

Make the most of your role model, because the top way kids learn is by *imitation*. The daily example you set in being interested in learning about the world around you, being persevering, patient, and optimistic about your challenges at work or home (including parenting!), will help your sons and daughters develop the determination to keep going on difficult math problems or other tasks despite frustrations.

Tap into Your Child's Center of Learning Excitement

What is your son or daughter most interested in? Is it whales, Civil War history, science fiction, cooking, computers, horses, or astronomy? Discovering and tapping into kids' special interests is a key to helping them become lifelong learners.

When they have their own "expert territory" or topic, hobby, or interest they know more about than anyone else in the family or classroom, their desire to learn accelerates. In addition, having an area of expertise can build self-worth and help a child overcome obstacles. It's a painless, effective way to help a child love to learn because you're plugging into something he wants to know.

You can begin to discover this center of learning excitement by asking questions, listening well, and noticing what your child gets excited about doing and takes pride in. You may need to be aware it might be something you have little or no interest in, so don't try to push him into the mold of what the rest of the family pursues or excels at.

Here are some good questions to discover your child's favorite interest:

- What do you like to do most?
- What do you think you're really good at?
- What do you enjoy doing most—at home or at school—that you'd do even if you didn't have to and it wasn't scheduled?
- What would you like to know more about?

The answers are clues to interests you can highlight and develop. What you're looking for is *what subject makes your children's eyes light up*. Once you find it, here are some things you could do to develop it and connect it with learning:

Provide resources like a subscription to a magazine on the subject of interest, books, or computer programs where they can learn more about it.

Take outings and day trips to hands-on science or living-history museums and other places that tap into kids' interests. Take them to live performances if they're interested in music; sit up close at the symphony and let them gaze into the orchestra pit to watch the conductor and musicians.

Find a class or summer camp in your community that is taught by someone who really knows this subject and can help them learn more. Examples include local art centers with Saturday classes and zoo internships for kids who are interested in animals. You can investigate courses on a variety of subjects that are offered to children and teens through 4-H clubs, YMCAs, universities, and community colleges.

Jenny, a fourth-grade girl I met when serving as an artist-in-residence, was fascinated with Arthurian legends, and after learning what she could in a unit and doing a project in social studies at her school, she still wanted to learn more. Jenny and her mom went to the library for more books, which spurred on her interest. Eventually her dad found a university professor who was willing to work with Jenny. Through e-mail and CD-ROMs the expert sent, he shared information he knew about Arthurian legends with Jenny, and eventually she majored in history in college. While we need to be very selective about the mentors we allow in our children's lives, qualified, trustworthy people of integrity who share their expertise and skills with our kids can help develop their interests and love of learning.

Boost Your Child's Learning Power
with Encouragement

As parents, we want our children to improve in their behavior, make good grades, and clean up their messy rooms. It's nice to have high expectations and goals for our kids, but sometimes our correction can turn into criticizing, and when this happens they don't get the encouragement they need. In fact, one study showed that moms tend to criticize their children 10 times more than they say a positive remark.

Consistent focusing on what our kids have done wrong rarely works to improve learning or motivation at school. Similarly, comparing them to a sibling ("If only you applied yourself like your sister!"), name-calling ("You are just lazy and childish"), and overreacting to mistakes are poor motivators.

Most children really want to please their parents, and discouragement and frustration set in when they think that no matter how hard they try, they won't be able to please Mom and Dad. Part of having a great support system at home (which children really need for the *long term*—12 years plus higher education) means building an environment of encouragement. It's important to establish a home base where kids know they're accepted and loved not just for *what they do* (their grades, soccer wins, and achievements) *but who they are* (the valuable person who is your son or daughter).

As John Drescher, a pastor and father of five, once said, "An ounce of praise can accomplish more than a ton of fault-finding."[3] We can always find fault since kids are works in progress, but encouragement to children is like sun and rain are to flowers—vital and necessary if they are going to grow and bloom as they were created to.

In fact, studies show that students who are successful learners have parents who are involved in their lives and have built strong, loving relationships with their kids, set limits, and spend time together. This is because emotional security (the foundation of which is a loving, trusting relationship with parents) is at the core of students' motivation systems and what experts call their "availability to learn." There's a high correlation between emotional insecurity and the turmoil it produces in a child's heart and mind, and his inability to learn in the classroom.

The opposite is also true, however. Encouraging children's efforts spurs on their learning. This is the good news! When a child grows up in a home with loving parents and an atmosphere of encouragement, it fosters mental growth. A good example of this is a young woman named Lana Israel who was awarded the highest honor for smart kids in England—"The Brain of England."

After the award ceremony, Lana was asked why she was such a great student and so successful in academics. She told about how her home was full of continual encouragement, where she and her sister didn't have to be perfect, and when they made mistakes, their parents encouraged them and believed in them. This encouraged Lana to take risks, try new courses of study, and use her creative abilities.

How can you apply this to your child and your home environment? When your daughter brings home a math test with a score of 82 (but you wish the grade were a 90), you could say, "That's a real improvement, honey; you got six points higher than last week." When her team doesn't win the debate, you could praise her efforts and the preparation that went into the event. When she does well and makes a high grade, praise *effort*, not just her intelligence. Research shows this stimulates more effort, but if we tell kids they are geniuses and the smartest person in the class and then they make a lower-than-expected grade, they'll reduce their efforts and thus learn less on the next unit of study.

One thing I learned in years and years of cheering for our three kids in their swim meets, volleyball and tennis matches, and baseball games is how very important momentum is to who wins the game. Education is like that too; it's a lot about momentum.

So, when the school year begins, getting off on the right foot is important. Meet the teacher and let her know you're involved in your child's education at home (as we've talked about in this book). Help your child get organized and use study methods that work for him and build on his strengths.

Then if a problem hits in math, science, writing, or another subject, you and your child tackle the problem together and come up with a solution to get her back on track. You don't waste time over-focusing on mistakes but notice what she's doing well or trying hard at and praise that. You don't have to wait until a special occasion or the highest score on the SAT is made to encourage the right actions. For instance, if your child has remembered to do his homework for five days and turned it in (quite a feat for some kids!), say, "You've been really responsible about your schoolwork this week" or "I'm happy about the effort you've put into your homework." In a sense, you become your child's best encourager because if you don't accept and encourage your kids, they'll find someone who will, and that person might encourage them to embrace values that you don't share.

You can also build momentum by looking for ways to tap into his center of learning excitement so his confidence and love of learning can build. As you apply these principles and ideas, positive momentum will grow as year by year your child develops the skills to be a life-long learner, equipped to succeed in school and life.

Let me encourage you along the way as you juggle work responsibilities, maintaining the household, and driving your kids to and from sports activities—keep believing in them, share their enthusiasm for learning and life, and most of all, *enjoy* their growing-up years—they fly by so quickly!

Pressing Questions
and
Practical Answers

Q: How valuable is a school's mission statement?

A: First, if you don't agree with or appreciate the emphasis of the school's mission statement, look for another school. Second, if it's a positive mission statement, then the philosophy is valuable only if the school has the leadership and programming to make sure the statement makes an impact in the lives of students. Examining whether or not the mission statement drives the school is a key to finding out if the leadership of the school can accomplish its goals.

To find out if the leadership is strong, you need to become a parent-collaborator and initiate discussion with the principal and teachers of the school. When interviewing the principal or teachers, ask specific questions based on objective results, not theory, such as, "Can you tell me about a program your school has developed that is designed to meet a goal of the mission statement?" "Can you tell me about a student whose character has been changed in a positive way because he or she is committed to the mission statement?" "Can you tell me how you've changed your curriculum to develop and fuel a passion for the school's mission statement?" "Can you tell me one way the mission statement has motivated you to stay at this school?"

Q: How much does student/teacher ratio matter? And how much should class size impact my decision about a particular school?

A: When researching a school, double-check and find out what the school means by "student/teacher ratio." This is not the same as class size. In general, small class size is your goal. A student/teacher ratio can include teachers your child may never have contact with, such as reading specialists or band instructors.

Common sense (as well as most research) tells us that the fewer students in a classroom, the more teacher contact the child will receive, and the younger the child the more important one-on-one contact with a teacher is. In public schools, the state or district usually sets the classroom limit, but in some schools principals still have some autonomy when determining class size. Ask the principal how she allocates teacher aides, determines when additional classroom teachers are hired to reduce class size, decides whether to hire classroom teachers or "specials" teachers, etc. In private school settings there are differing standards, so be sure to ask about maximum class sizes.

Next, determine your child's needs. If he is able to focus and is an independent and confident learner, then class size is less important than if your child has trouble focusing or noise distracts him from the task of learning. Does your child need to hear instructions several times or is he able to listen and work unsupervised? Does your child need lots of affirmation? The answers to these questions and others like them will help you establish priorities and decide if you need to find a school with small class sizes. Is this one of your non-negotiables?

The ultimate low classroom size is usually found in homeschool settings. If this is a key factor for you, consider researching that option.

Q: What is the significance of the number of children at a school who are on a free/reduced lunch program?

A: You need to evaluate this number in light of the larger community in order to determine if this is a significant factor or not. You may face challenges if the school is serving a disproportionate share of children from financially disadvantaged homes. If this is the case, investigate at the district level to find out more about the school's population. By federal law, public schools are held accountable for their academic standards regardless of the number of low-income students who attend them.

When comparing schools, studies show money does make a difference—but overall test scores should be considered as well. Many schools that have children on free/reduced lunch plans teach to the high end of the spectrum and may be a good option for your children.

Q: Is it important for schools to allow parents to be a part of the hiring process for new teachers?

A: This is not the norm—but if the school or principal does let parents have a voice in teacher selection, it's a good thing. When a school welcomes parental involvement, it is usually a sign of great communication and a commitment to serving the community. It will make your job of parent-collaborator easier.

Q: Should I consider the school's discipline system before selecting a school?

A: Yes! Examine this issue carefully. It's usually a non-negotiable for most take-charge parents. Your child deserves a safe environment, but even the best school will have some students with discipline problems. Some key factors in evaluating a good discipline system are: (1) a well-defined discipline philosophy. All staff should be trained in the procedures and all students should be held equally accountable; (2) a progressive level of discipline with an emphasis on instruction for the students. There should be rewards for good behavior as well as consequences for poor behavior; (3) discipline procedures should be in accord with your family's biblical values, age appropriate, and follow state and federal mandates; and (4) stiff penalties for illegal substance abuse or violent or dangerous behavior. The popular term today is "zero tolerance," but you may want to evaluate if the school distinguishes between a child who brings an aspirin to school in his pocket and another who was caught smoking marijuana.

If you are considering a private school that uses corporal punishment, make sure you are comfortable with the procedures and that there is a clear and consistent written policy. Ask questions such as, "Will I be notified before corporal punishment is used on my child as a disciplinary measure?" "Will two or more staff members be present for accountability?" "Is it permissible that my child be exempt from corporal punishment if I so wish it?"

Q: How important is it for my child to be taught creation or "intelligent design" as opposed to evolution?

A: No matter what children are taught in school, it's the parents' responsibility to make sure their children understand the biblical perspective on creation. You may not feel qualified to teach it, but you can ask your pastor or other respected Christian leaders for help in finding resources to help you in this goal. Due to the controversial nature of the topic, Focus on the Family encourages each family, in conjunction with their church, to make its own decision regarding the interpretation of the book of Genesis; however, all children should learn that evolution is a theory, not fact, and that the theory has many flaws; these flaws have not been adequately addressed in the 150 years since Darwin introduced the theory.

If you have high school students, one thing to consider when selecting science curriculum is the college application process. Some California public universities are rejecting the science credits of high school graduates who attended private Christian schools and used texts that taught "intelligent design." There is still much work to be done on encouraging colleges to honor Christian students' equal-access rights, so be proactive and keep on top of what is happening in your state by watching the news and maintaining contact with the school science teachers; you should not change what you think your child needs to learn in science class, but be shrewd in how you go about it so that it won't lead to surprises or cause trouble down the academic road.

Q: I'm worried that if I put my daughter in a public school, she will be taught that homosexuality is normal, healthy, and worthy of being embraced.

A: This is a valid concern even for parents of kindergarten students. By gathering information and becoming a parent-collaborator and parent-coach, you may be able to eliminate or mitigate most of this teaching. You will need to investigate to what extent "tolerance for homosexuality" is being taught at the public school you are considering. Contact members of the school board and find out if there is one who shares your concerns. Ask friends and neighbors to help you find a concerned Christian teacher in your district and keep in touch with him or her regarding these issues. The pro-homosexual content can be buried in textbooks and/or be a part of "multiculturalism," "diversity," or sex education. Be alert and know who the guest speakers will be in your children's classrooms or assemblies.

If there is objectionable material being presented, you will need to set up a discussion with the school's principal to find out if your daughter can receive alternative assignments, lectures, or books. Ask that she be pulled from specific programs that you are not comfortable with. (Some state courts are making this more and more difficult and are ruling that parents may not interfere with the public school's job. Keep abreast of what is going on in your state.) How the principal deals with your concerns will probably tell you if you want to enroll your daughter in that school or not.

Q: Does a school's reading program really matter to my child?

A: Maybe—it depends on your child's reading aptitude. Nationwide roughly 30 percent of children can learn to read efficiently with either a whole-language or a phonics-based program. Another 30 percent will need some phonics instruction to learn to decode, and the rest of the students will need individual help. Keep a watch on your child and make sure he reads at grade level, if not a year ahead. If your child needs help, take action or hire a tutor sooner rather than later. The earlier he overcomes reading disabilities the better.

The main factor to consider is the school's overall reading score. If few kids are reading at an advanced level, this is a forecast for trouble. It means the school is not preparing students to read; as the children move through the system, they are not able to keep up with textbooks and the material is "dumbed down." Even if your child can read well, being in a classroom with a majority of peers who can't may be detrimental in the long run.

Q: My son is an average student, and yet I want him to take Advanced Placement or honors courses in high school. Is this wise?

A: Maybe. This goal will require you to blend your roles as a critical decision maker and a parent-coach. First, you need to find out what requirements are needed before your son can be enrolled. Some AP or honors-track courses are available only through an application process. He may need prerequisite classes. If your son qualifies for the advanced track, it could be a great thing for him to be challenged academically. Who knows—rising to the level of more difficult course work may bring out a new scholastic passion. Additionally, a lot of students in high-end courses are high achievers and good students; being around a positive peer group could be a huge benefit to your son.

Next, think like a parent-coach. Evaluate the situation carefully before you insist he take the courses, because it could put a wedge in your relationship. If your son is not ready or can't handle the workload of an AP or honors class, don't despair. Kids mature at differing rates. High school is not a race, and while you want your son to get the best education possible, there are other factors you should consider, such as making sure he has enough time for his other interests, spiritual training, friends, and family. Also, there is a chance he may not perform well in the AP or honors courses—you need to consider if he can rebound from a failure.

Q: How important is having extra resources for remedial help, special needs, or tutoring programs at a school?

A: This should be part of your consideration before choosing a school. If extra resources are not available, you'll have to hire tutors or find support elsewhere. Consider extra services a plus, even for gifted students. You may not believe your child needs extra services today, but she could in the future. For example, high school honors student Danielle could whip up A's in all her subjects until she took Spanish I. Suddenly her natural aptitudes were challenged, and she needed academic help for the first time. The school she attended did not offer any support, and the teacher was not available after school because she had younger children waiting for her at home. Danielle's parents did not know Spanish, so they had to pay a private tutor to help their daughter learn the material and keep up her grade point average. It was costly, but worth it.

If you have children who need help in reading it could take a year or longer to get them caught up. (See page 193.) How well are you equipped to train your child in phonics and fluency? Can you afford a private tutor?

If your child has severe academic/learning challenges or special needs, you will want to consider the high financial cost of extra support. Public schools are required by law to provide special services for qualified students—for many families with a special-needs child, public schools are the only realistic option.

Q: I have an option of sending my child to a good charter school, but the bus ride is 45 minutes long, one way. Does that sound reasonable?

A: Many charter schools don't have buses, so even having the option is a good thing. Factors to consider include the bus environment, the child's age and temperament, and how long you are willing to be separated from your child. Ask yourself: *Can my child do homework on the bus? Will the long ride interfere with extracurricular activities? How good/bad are my other school options? If the bus situation doesn't work out, am I able and willing to drive? Can my child handle being gone from home for so long? Is the atmosphere on the bus healthy for my child?*

Not all decisions in regard to school choice are easy; sometimes making sacrifices is necessary. You are looking for the most successful school choice, not a perfect, easy situation. Only you, the parent as a critical decision maker, are qualified to determine what is a reasonable sacrifice for your family to make in order to get the best education possible for your child.

Q: My son's middle school is going to the block system. Should I be concerned?

A: As a take-charge parent, you should be concerned about every factor that can impact your son's education success. Block systems extend the time a student is in one class session. Begin making your decision by asking teachers how they plan on using the extended class time; they may be able to do more hands-on projects in the new system, a plus for wiggly, kinesthetic learners. Fill out the chart in chapter 8, taking into consideration your child's learning style and academic needs, and then decide if your son should stay at that school. You may find that with some adjustments and a take-charge attitude, you can help your son thrive in the block-system setting.

Q: My daughter is being bullied at school. Should I move her to a new school?

A: Removing your child from the school is definitely an option, but remember, other schools will very likely have bullies too.

What can you do? According to Focus on the Family's book *Help! My Child Is Being Bullied,* awareness is a major factor in solving the problem. Get involved and become a take-charge parent. Bullying should be taken seriously. Find out what the school's policy is on bullying. Different schools take different approaches. Does your child's school have adequate adult supervision in and outside the classroom (hall monitors, lunchroom monitors, class helpers, playground supervisors, etc.)? What is the discipline procedure for a bully? Will both sets of parents be involved immediately? Ask questions and don't be afraid to follow up with the teacher, school counselor, and/or principal. You have a right to know what's being done to protect your child. If the school administration is unable to resolve the problem, depending on the severity of the situation, you may need to go to the police or a higher district official.[1]

Q: How big a school is too big?

A. That depends on your child's needs. A big school is not necessarily a bad thing. Larger schools typically offer more sports, music, enrichment, and arts opportunities. Your child may need the depth and breadth of curriculum a large school can offer. Larger schools can sometimes accommodate your special-needs child better because the staff will be larger and the collective experience of the teachers greater.

You may have several first-grade teachers as a pool to choose from, where in a small school, there may be only one or two instructors. At the high school level, a large school may bring more opportunities for state and nationwide recognition for your high-achieving offspring.

The physical building and how classes are set up are key factors in determining whether or not your child can succeed in a large school. Consider the buildings. Can your child get from class to class within the designated time? Will she have time for a locker stop or to use the restroom, or will she be running down the hallways after each class? What about after-school pickup? Is the parking adequate? Are the buses safe and efficient? Is there adequate supervision in the hallways and on the playground? For elementary schools, consider the kindergarten area. Is there a safe and separate play area for the little ones to use?

At a smaller school, it would probably be easier to meet people and develop community. At a large school, however, there are a greater number of families and therefore a larger pool to search through to find like-minded friends.

A take-charge parent can make the most of a large school situation. As with any other schooling option, you'll have to decide if you can live with the drawbacks of being in a large school, but you should also have the confidence that if it's the best choice for your child, the effort you put into helping your child succeed is more important than the school choice.

Q: I want to homeschool, but I'm afraid of burning out. Is it really as much work as I imagine?

A: Parenting is rarely easy. Supporting a child in any education program requires time and effort, but especially with homeschooling. There are, however, ways to minimize the stress of homeschooling, and there are several good resources to help you. (See chapter 12.)

If you believe homeschooling is the best option for your child, that conviction should help fuel your passion. Consider virtual academies and support groups—they can help lighten the academic and organization load. Become a take-charge parent and determine ways you can make homeschooling work for you while still maintaining a healthy family atmosphere. For example, when you homeschool, you can set your own schedule so that if your family needs a break from academics, you can take it. That's the beauty of the homeschool experience—you can tailor the program to accommodate your family's needs.

Resources to Help with Your Child's Education

General Education

Every Child Can Succeed: Making the Most of Your Child's Learning Style, by Cynthia Ulrich Tobias (Focus on the Family, 1999).
School Choices: What's Best for Your Child?, by Jan Sheble (Beacon Hill Press, 2003).
School Starts at Home, by Cheri Fuller (Pinon Press, 2004),
Surviving Middle School: How to Manage the Maze, by Sandy Silverthorne (Standard Publishing, 2003).
Talkers, Watchers, and Doers: Unlocking Your Child's Unique Learning Style by Cheri Fuller (Pinon Press, 2004).
The Way They Learn, by Cynthia Ulrich Tobias (Focus on the Family, 1998).

General Parenting

Bringing Out the Best in Your Child: 80 Ways to Focus on Every Kid's Strengths, by Cynthia Ulrich Tobias and Carol Funk (Servant Publications, 1997).
Bringing Up Boys, by Dr. James Dobson (Tyndale, 2005).
Giving Your Child the Excellence Edge: 10 Traits Your Child Needs to Achieve Lifelong Success, by Vicki Caruana (Tyndale, 2004).
Growing Compassionate Kids: Helping Kids See Beyond Their Backyard, by Jan Johnson (Upper Room Books, 2001).
Home Court Advantage: Preparing Your Children to Be Winners in Life, by Kevin Leman (Tyndale, 2005).

Moms on the Job: 7 Secrets for Success at Home and Work, by Sabrina
   O'Malone (Tyndale, 2006).
The New Dare to Discipline, by Dr. James Dobson (Tyndale, 1996).
The New Strong-Willed Child, by Dr. James Dobson (Tyndale, 2004).
Raising Motivated Kids, by Cheri Fuller (Pinon Press, 2004).
*Seven Habits of a Healthy Home: Preparing the Ground in Which
   Your Children Can Grow,* by Bill Carmichael (VMI Publishing,
   2002).
*A Special Kind of Love: For Those Who Love Children with Special
   Needs,* by Susan Titus Osborn and Janet Lynn Mitchell (Broad-
   man & Holman, 2004).

Homeschooling

*Help for the Harried Homeschooler: A Practical Guide to Balancing
   Your Child's Education with the Rest of Your Life,* by Christine M.
   Field (Shaw, 2002).
*Help! I'm Married to a Homeschooling Mom: Showing Dads How to
   Meet the Needs of Their Homeschooling Wives,* by Todd Wilson
   (Moody Publishers, 2004).
Homeschooling on a Shoestring: A Jam-Packed Guide for Parents, by
   Melissa L. Morgan and Judith Waite Allee (Shaw, 2000).
*So You're Thinking About Homeschooling: Fifteen Families Show How
   You Can Do It!,* by Lisa Whelchel (Multnomah, 2003).
The Ultimate Guide to Homeschooling, by Debra Bell (Thomas
   Nelson, 2005).

Single Parenting

Going It Alone: Meeting the Challenges of Being a Single Mom, by Michele Howe (Hendrickson Publishers, 1999).
Successful Single Parenting, by Gary Richmond (Harvest House Publishers, 1998).

Social Issues

A Chicken's Guide to Talking Turkey with Your Kids About Sex, by Kevin Leman and Kathy Flores Bell (Zondervan, 2004).
"Dear Parents: What Your Teens Need to Know About Sex" by Linda Klepacki. http://www.pureintimacy.org/cs/parents/raising_children/a0000167.cfm
How and When to Tell Your Kids About Sex: A Lifelong Approach to Shaping Your Child's Sexual Character, by Stanton L. Jones and Brenna B. Jones (NavPress Publishing Group, 1993).
How to Drugproof Your Kids: Steering Children Away from the Harmful Use of Drugs (Focus on the Family, 2005).
How to Stay Christian in College, by Jay Budziszewski (Th1nk Books, 2004).
How to Stay Christian in High School, by Steve Gerali (Th1nk Books, 2004).
How to Talk to Your Kids About Sexuality, by David Scherrer and Linda Klepacki (Cook Communications, 2004).
"Teaching Captivity?" a booklet that explores how the pro-gay agenda is affecting our schools, and how you can make a differ-

ence. To request this booklet, call 1-800-A-FAMILY (232-6459) and ask for item XY132. Suggested donation, $3.

"Straight Answers: Exposing the Myths and Facts About Homosexuality" To request this booklet, call 1-800-A-FAMILY (232-6459) and ask for item, XY112. Suggested donation, $3.

Spiritual Training Helps for Teens

Dare 2 Share: A Field Guide to Sharing Your Faith, by Greg Stier (Tyndale, 2006).

Fuel: 10-Minute Devotions to Ignite the Faith of Parents and Teens, by Joe White (Tyndale, 2003).

Stand: Core Truths You Must Know for an Unshakable Faith, by Alex McFarland (Tyndale, 2005).

Spiritual Training Helps for Parents

How to Lead Your Child to Christ, by Robert Wolgemuth and Bobbie Wolgemuth (Tyndale, 2005).

The Key to Your Child's Heart, by Gary Smalley (W Publishing Group, 2003).

Lead Your Teen to a Lifelong Faith, by Joe White and Jim Weidmann (Tyndale, 2005).

Parents' Guide to the Spiritual Growth of Children, edited by John Trent, Ph.D., Rick Osborne, and Kurt Bruner (Tyndale, 2000).

Parents' Guide to the Spiritual Mentoring of Teens, edited by Jim Weidmann and Joe White (Tyndale, 2000).

Soundbites from Heaven: What God Wants Us to Hear When We Talk to Our Kids, by Rachael Carman (Focus on the Family, 2005).

Teaching Kids About God: An Age-By-Age Plan for Parents of Children from Birth to Age Twelve, by various authors (Tyndale, 2003).

Websites

www.citizenlink.com (look for the education-issues analysis section) www.ed.gov/nclb/overview/intro/parents/parentsfacts.html (look for the education-issues analysis section)

Search for the following organizations for private Christian schools:

American Association of Christian Schools
Association of Christian Schools International
Association of Classical Christian Schools
National Christian School Association

Search for the following organizations for homeschool help:

American Homeschool Association
National Home Education Network
National Homeschool Association
Virtual Homeschool International

To help research your public schools, start with a search for the following organizations:
Department of Education
National Center for Education Statistics
School Accountability Report—by state
State Department of Education
The Heritage Foundation

Notes

Chapter 1: A New Day

1. ED.Gov, U.S. Department of Education, *A Guide to Education* and No Child Left Behind, http://www.ed.gov/nclb/ overview/intro/guide/guide_pg6.html#fnref11; National Center for Education Statistics, *1.1 Million Homeschooled Students in the United States in 2003*, http://nces.ed.gov/nhes/ homeschool/: CAPE, Council for American Private Education, Private School Statistics at a Glance, http://www.capenet.org/ facts.html

2. Laurence Steinberg, *Beyond the Classroom: Why School Reform Has Failed and What Parents Need to Do* (New York: Touchstone, 1996), p. 14.

3. *Digest of Education Statistics 2001*, February 2002, National Center for Education Statistics.

4. *Violence in American Schools*, 1998, reprint 2003. Cambridge University Press, Press Syndicate of University of Cambridge, Pitt Building, Trumpington Street, Cambridge, UK.

Chapter 2: The Changing Face of Education

1. Indiana University, "History of the American Classroom: A Brief History of Public Education in the United States," http://www.indiana.edu/~w505a/bennett.html#A%20Brief%20History.

2. Ibid.

3. USINFO.STATE.GOV, "The Northwest Ordinance (1787)," http://usinfo.state.gov/usa/infousa/facts/democrac/5.htm.

4. Boston Public Schools, "The English High School History," http://www.boston.k12.ma.us/english/alumni/EHS history.htm.

5. Diane Ravitch, *Left Back: A Century of Failed School Reforms* (New York: Simon & Schuster, 2000), p. 16.

6. IES National Center for Education Statistics, "Fast Facts," http://nces.ed.gov/fastfacts/display.asp?r=76.4097859064648& svr=3&id=66.

7. ED.gov, U.S. Department of Education, "A Nation at Risk," http://www.ed.gov/pubs/NatAtRisk/risk.html.

8. ED.gov, U.S. Department of Education, "A Nation at Risk," http://www.ed.gov/pubs/NatAtRisk/findings.html.

9. ED.gov, U.S. Department of Education, "A Nation at Risk," http://www.ed.gov/pubs/NatAtRisk/risk.html.

10. Chester Finn, "A Nation Still at Risk," *Commentary*, (May 1989), pp. 17-23.

11. IES National Center for Education Statistics, "Estimated federal on-budget funds for education, by agency: Fiscal year 2003," http://nces.ed.gov/quicktables/Detail.asp?Key=1216.

12. Laurence Steinberg, *Beyond the Classroom: Why School Reform Has Failed and What Parents Need to Do* (New York: Simon & Schuster, 1996), p. 67.

13. Ibid.

14. Krista Kafer, The Heritage Foundation, "Policy Research and Analysis," http://www.heritage.org/Research/Education/WM127.cfm.

15. PBS, "School: The Story of American Education (Evolving Classroom)," http://www.pbs.org/kcet/publicschool/evolving_classroom.

Chapter 3: The Take-Charge Parent

1. C. S. Lewis, *The Four Loves* (New York: Harcourt Brace, 1960), p. 76.

2. Laurence Steinberg, *Beyond the Classroom: Why School Reform Has Failed and What Parents Need to Do* (New York: Simon & Schuster, 1996), p. 187.

3. Ibid.

4. Ibid.

5. Ibid.

6. Ibid.

7. Action Alliance for Children, "Schools that Welcome Parents," http://www.4children.org/news/101sche.htm.
8. The Free Dictionary, "Champion," http://www.thefree dictionary.com/champion.
9. Gerard Manley Hopkins, "The Principle or Foundation," http://www.spirithome.com/workspir.html.

Chapter 4: How to Create Success in Today's Educational Environment

1. Dr. Kevin Leman, *Home Court Advantage* (Carol Stream, IL: Tyndale, 2005), p. 46.
2. Laurence Steinberg, *Beyond the Classroom: Why School Reform Has Failed and What Parents Need to Do* (New York: Simon & Schuster, 1996), pp. 24-25.
3. Caroline Hoxby, "If Families Matter Most, Where Do Schools Come In?" in T. Moe, ed., *A Primer on America's Schools* (Stanford, CA: Hoover Institution Press, 2001), p. 97.
4. David J. Armor, *Maximizing Intelligence* (New Brunswick, NJ: Transaction Publishers 2003), pp. 51-100.

Chapter 5: The Pros and Cons of Today's School Choices

1. Paul Hill, "What Is Public About Public Education," in T. Moe, ed., *A Primer on America's Schools* (Stanford, CA: Hoover Institution Press, 2001), p. 289.

2. Paul Hill, "Choice in American Education," in T. Moe, ed., *A Primer on America's Schools* (Stanford, CA: Hoover Institution Press, 2001), p. 249.

Chapter 6: My Child's Learning Style and Best Learning Environment

1. For more information on Schools Attuned, which are based on over 25 years of work by Dr. Mel Levine, his colleagues at the Clinical Center for the Study of Development and Learning at the University of North Carolina School of Medicine in Chapel Hill, North Carolina, and other researchers in the field, see www.allkindsofminds.org or write Schools Attuned, P.O. Box 3580, Chapel Hill, NC 27515.

2. Jim Trelease, "Turning On the Turned Off Reader," audiotape (Springfield, MA: Reading Tree Productions).

Chapter 10: Equipping Your Child for Lifelong Learning and Success

1. Karen Guzman, "Whose homework is it?" *The News & Observer,* Charlotte, NC, May 3, 2005, Section E, pp. 1-3.

2. Dr. Judy Abbott, Assistant Professor of Education at West Virginia University. Research and dissertation underscoring the importance of parents in encouraging children to write at home, 1996.

3. John Drescher, *Seven Things Children Need* (Scottsdale, PA: Herald Press, 1976), p. 94.

Chapter 11: Pressing Questions
and Practical Answers

1. Excerpted and adapted from Bill Maier, ed., *Help! My Child Is Being Bullied!* (Carol Stream, IL: Tyndale, 2006), pp. 35-38.

About the Authors

Maria Hernandez Ferrier, General Editor

For three decades Maria Hernandez Ferrier, Ed.D. has been an education leader at the community, state, and national levels. From 2002-2005 she worked for the U.S. Department of Education, being promoted to the position of Assistant Deputy Secretary.

In the fall of 2002, Dr. Ferrier began the now annual "Celebrating Our Rising Stars," a national summit for educators, parents, and community leaders interested in English language learners and their families. Dr. Ferrier was appointed as the co-chair of the Hispanic Association of Colleges and Universities (HACU), National Leadership Team, a group of college and university presidents representing Hispanic-serving institutions and several senior level managers. Maria also initiated the formation of the department's faith-based Hispanic task force. The mission of the task force was to reach and apprise parents of English language learners of their rights and opportunities under the new educational federal law.

Dr. Ferrier's accomplishments include the creation, development, and/or implementation of highly successful programs, among them the first elementary chapter of Students Against Drunk Driving in the U.S. Many of these programs have served as models and have been replicated in schools in Texas as well as in other states. She currently serves as an executive director for the Southwest (San Antonio) Independent School District.

■ ■ ■

Marc Fey is the director of Community Impact Outreach at Focus on the Family, overseeing the groundbreaking Christian worldview program, *Focus on the Family's The Truth Project.* He has also served as Focus's education analyst, where his 10 years of experience as a high school English teacher in California public schools informed his commentary on education issues and the family. Marc's experience as a pastor, teacher, and Focus on the Family director shapes his work with leaders, families, and young people. Most of all, he enjoys time with his wife; two sons, ages 13 and 15; and daughter, age 6.

■ ■ ■

Cheri Fuller is an international speaker and author of over 30 books, including *Raising Motivated Kids, The Mom You're Meant to Be,* and *School Starts at Home.* Cheri has taught at every level from elementary school to college. A former Oklahoma Mother of the Year, she has appeared on national TV and radio programs and is a popular conference speaker. She and her husband live in Oklahoma, and have three married children and six grandchildren. Her Web site, www.cherifuller.com, contains many resources for moms, dads, teachers, and churches.

■ ■ ■

Charles W. Johnson graduated from Westmont College in Santa Barbara, California, with a B.A. in English and history. He also earned an M.A. in Pupil Personnel Services from Point Loma University. During an 18-year career in education, Chuck Johnson was a teacher, counselor, and assistant principal of curriculum at San Marino High School in the Los Angeles area and the principal of Huntington (Middle) School in the same district. In 1992, Chuck joined the staff of Focus on the Family and became the founding editor of *Teachers in Focus*. After five years in that position, he became the editorial director for the Focus periodicals department that created 13 distinct and segmented publications (both magazines and newsletters). In 2004, he joined the staff at Covenant Village of Turlock (California) as associate administrator for residential living. He is also the president of the Evangelical Press Association, a national organization of Christian periodicals publishers. He has been married to his wife, Gwen, for nearly 30 years, and they have two grown children. Following their graduations from college, their son, Todd, worked as a teacher and a behavioral therapist and their daughter, Jenny, is teaching fifth graders in Southern California.

■ ■ ■

Jim Mhoon has dedicated his adult life to serving families. For over 16 years, he worked in several roles at Focus on the Family including that of program director for parenting ministries. Currently, he serves as vice president of marketing and communication for CRISTA

Ministries, an organization that, among other activities, runs private Christian schools in the greater Seattle area. Jim holds an M.B.A. in Business Administration and a B.A. in psychology. He is married with two children, including a son with multiple special needs.

■ ■ ■

Susan Martins Miller is the author of more than 40 books for children and adults. Her works include both fiction and nonfiction. She contributes on a regular basis to publications that are used in teaching children to know Jesus and grow to be like Him. These include children's sermons, creative Sunday school lessons, and resources for family ministry. Susan is a graduate of Westmont College in Santa Barbara, California, and holds an M.A. from Trinity Evangelical Divinity School in Deerfield, Illinois. In addition to writing, she has conducted workshops for writers and editors in Nepal, India, Slovakia, Colombia, and Bolivia. She lives in Colorado with her husband and children.

FOCUS ᴼᴺ THE FAMILY®

Welcome to the family!

Whether you purchased this book, borrowed it, or received it as a gift, we're glad you're reading it. It's just one of the many helpful, encouraging, and biblically based resources produced by Focus on the Family for people in all stages of life.

Focus began in 1977 with the vision of one man, Dr. James Dobson, a licensed psychologist and author of numerous best-selling books on marriage, parenting, and family. Alarmed by the societal, political, and economic pressures that were threatening the existence of the American family, Dr. Dobson founded Focus on the Family with one employee and a once-a-week radio broadcast aired on 36 stations.

Now an international organization reaching millions of people daily, Focus on the Family is dedicated to preserving values and strengthening and encouraging families through the life-changing message of Jesus Christ.

Focus on the Family Magazines

These faith-building, character-developing publications address the interests, issues, concerns, and challenges faced by every member of your family from preschool through the senior years.

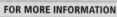

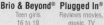

| Focus on the Family **Citizen®** U.S. news issues | Focus on the Family **Clubhouse Jr.™** Ages 4 to 8 | Focus on the Family **Clubhouse™** Ages 8 to 12 | **Breakaway®** Teen guys | **Brio®** Teen girls 12 to 16 | **Brio & Beyond®** Teen girls 16 to 19 | **Plugged In®** Reviews movies, music, TV |

BP06XFM

More Great Resources
from Focus on the Family®

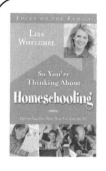

So You're Thinking about Homeschooling
By Lisa Whelchel
Lisa Whelchel—herself a homeschooling mother of three—uses fifteen portraits of homeschooling families to show how every family can successfully face the unique challenges of its situation. Seeing a wide variety of homeschooling families in action gives you, the parent, information and confidence to make your own decisions about home-based education.

The Way They Learn
By Cynthia Ulrich Tobias
In this enlightening resource, Cynthia Ulrich Tobias introduced the variety of learning styles that shape the way students interpret their world. Once these approaches are understood, parents and teachers can become far more effective in helping children grasp confusing concepts, stay interested in lessons, and utilize their strengths.

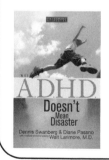

Why ADHD Doesn't Mean Disaster
By Dennis Swanberg, Dr. Walt Larimore & Diane Passno
Why ADHD Doesn't Mean Disaster provides a realistic, encouraging perspective from parents who have raised children with ADHD, as well as some who have ADHD themselves. Filled with insights, personal stories and sound medical expertise, this book gives parents facing the challenges of handling ADHD hope that breaks through the hype.

FOR MORE INFORMATION

 Online:
Log on to www.family.org
In Canada, log on to www.focusonthefamily.ca.

 Phone:
Call toll free: (800) A-FAMILY
In Canada, call toll free: (800) 661-9800.

BP06XP1